DO
CAMPAIGNS
MATTER?

Contemporary American Politics

The **Contemporary American Politics** series is intended to assist students and faculty in the field of American politics by bridging the gap between advanced but oft-times impenetrable research on the one hand, but oversimplified presentations on the other. The volumes in this series represent the most exciting work in political science—cutting-edge research that focuses on major unresolved questions, contradicts conventional wisdom, or initiates new areas of investigation. Ideal as supplemental texts for undergraduate courses, these volumes will examine the institutions, processes, and policy questions that make up the American political landscape.

Books in This Series

DO CAMPAIGNS MATTER?
Thomas M. Holbrook

GENDER DYNAMICS IN CONGRESSIONAL ELECTIONS
Richard Logan Fox

THOMAS M. HOLBROOK

DO CAMPAIGNS MATTER?

CONTEMPORARY
AMERICAN
POLITICS

SAGE Publications
International Educational and Professional Publisher
Thousand Oaks London New Delhi

For information address:

 SAGE Publications, Inc.
2455 Teller Road
Thousand Oaks, California 91320
E-mail: order@sagepub.com

SAGE Publications Ltd.
6 Bonhill Street
London EC2A 4PU
United Kingdom

SAGE Publications India Pvt. Ltd.
M-32 Market
Greater Kailash I
New Delhi 110 048 India

Printed in the United States of America

Library of Congress Cataloging-in-Publication Data

Holbrook, Thomas M.
    Do campaigns matter? / author, Thomas M. Holbrook.
        p.   cm. — (Contemporary American politics)
    Includes bibliographical references and index.
    ISBN 0-8039-7344-6 (cloth: acid-free paper). —
    ISBN 0-8039-7345-4 (pbk.: acid-free paper)
        1. Presidents—United States—Election. 2. Electioneering—
    United States. 3. Voting—United States. I. Title. II. Series.
    JK524.H65 1996   96-4469

This book is printed on acid-free paper.

96 97 98 99 10 9 8 7 6 5 4 3 2 1

Sage Production Editor: Gillian Dickens
Sage Typesetter: Janelle LeMaster

This book is dedicated to the memory
of my friend, colleague, and mentor,
Charley Tidmarch.

Contents

Series Editor's Introduction

This new Sage series on Contemporary American Politics is intended to convey the most exciting work in political science—"cutting-edge research focusing on major unresolved questions or research that contradicts conventional wisdom or that initiates entirely new areas of investigation." In this respect, Thomas Holbrook's *Do Campaigns Matter?* represents a great beginning. In the past several decades of work on voting and elections, little attention has been paid to the campaigns themselves. Occasionally, explicit statements have suggested that the campaign has had only a negligible effect on the voters; more often, there was simply puzzlement—wonderment at how much attention parties and candidates paid to the campaign when we were unable to demonstrate that it had much effect. Holbrook's book breaks that mold, demonstrating that campaigns have a variety of effects on voters.

Do Campaigns Matter? is also an excellent beginning in another sense. The series is intended to convey cutting-edge research in a style that "bridges the gap between advanced, but sometimes impenetrable research and understandable [though] greatly simplified presentations." Holbrook does not shy away from complex ideas and materials, but his findings are presented in a way that is accessible to readers at various levels of learning in regard to statistical skills.

One important feature of Holbrook's work is his innovative combination of a variety of kinds of data about the campaign, including trial heats, a record of important campaign events, newspaper reports about the campaign, and surveys of voter behavior. By combining these elements, Holbrook paints a more realistic picture of campaigns and of their effects than is possible with only one or two kinds of data.

As yet another long presidential campaign is upon us, we are delighted to inaugurate our series with a volume that shows that all our collective efforts are not without consequence. Presidential campaigns do matter; it is surprising that we had to wait so many years for political scientists to recognize that fact.

—*Richard G. Niemi*

Preface

I began thinking about the ideas presented in this book several years ago, when I was a graduate student at the University of Iowa. In fact, I considered writing my dissertation on the effect of campaigns on presidential elections. There was one small problem, however: I didn't have the foggiest idea about how one would go about assessing the effect of campaigns. I think, and I hope the reader agrees, that I have finally figured out at least one way of assessing the effect of campaigns.

Having cut my teeth on economic voting and election forecasting models, I originally approached the topic as a bit of a nonbeliever. When I first began to mull over the issues addressed in this book, I was convinced that campaigns were virtually irrelevant to election outcomes. Given the apparent ability of simple forecast models to accurately predict election outcomes and the impressive performance of individual-level voting models, I did not see any room for campaigns to exert an independent influence on elections. By the time I finally started this project, however, I had come around to a point of view that could best be classified as agnostic: I had been impressed enough by anecdotal evidence of campaign effects that I was at least keeping an open mind to the possibility of campaign effects. By the end of this project, I became persuaded that "something is out there." I think the evidence in this book clearly shows that although campaigns may not be the most important determinant of presidential election outcomes, they certainly play a key role in shaping public opinion and, ultimately, influencing outcomes.

A number of people have either directly or indirectly influenced this project and, hence, deserve to be thanked. First, I owe a debt of gratitude to those individuals who helped shape my approach to political science, my teachers at the University of Iowa. I especially want to thank Mike Lewis-Beck, Doug Madsen, Peter Snow, and Art Miller for what they taught me. I also need to thank those who commented on some of my earlier work on presidential campaigns: Jim Stimson, Ken Meier, Jim Garand, John Bibby, and Charley Tidmarch. I am also grateful for the comments provided by anonymous reviewers at various journals and publishers that either accepted or rejected my earlier efforts in this area. Almost without exception, I have found their comments useful.

My colleagues at UWM deserve thanks for their support of my research program over the years, as well as for their friendship. Thanks go especially to my colleague, Steve Percy, who always manages to convince me, by example, that I'm really not that busy after all. In addition, I would like to thank Linda Hawkins and the staff of the Social Science Research Facility for their assistance in getting the data onto my mainframe account so I could use it.

I also owe a debt of gratitude to Nicole Johnson, a graduate student at UWM, who spent countless hours coding the media coverage data that play a central role in Chapters 3 and 4.

I also need to thank the Inter-University Consortium for Political and Social Research (ICPSR) and the Center for Political Studies (CPS) at the University of Michigan. Many of the data analyzed in this book were made available by the ICPSR and the CPS. The support provided by institutions such as the ICPSR and the CPS makes it possible for others in the scholarly community, such as myself, to pursue large-scale independent research projects.

The organizers (The National Election Studies and the Annenberg School of Communication) and participants of the Conference on the Impact of Presidential Campaigns are largely responsible for restarting my intellectual engine at a time when I needed a boost. This book was essentially idle for a three-month period before I attended the conference. I came home from the conference with a fresh perspective and a clearer idea of what issues a book on campaigns should address. Therefore, I thank all who participated in the conference.

A number of other people have had a more direct effect on the work done in this book. First, Dick Niemi and Barbara Sinclair, coeditors of the Sage series, have provided invaluable input throughout this process. Their thorough evaluation of the manuscript and helpful suggestions have made this a much better book than it would otherwise have been. I also want to thank John Aldrich of Duke University, whose first-rate review of this book provided a number of useful insights and comments, many of which were incorporated into the manuscript. Also, David Farrell of the University of Manchester was generous enough to read the entire manuscript and share his insights with me. I can honestly say that all of the advice I received from these people was useful and led to a better manuscript.

I would like to thank the University of Wisconsin Press for granting permission to use a limited amount of material from "Campaigns, National Conditions, and U.S. Presidential Elections," an article that I published in the *American Journal of Political Science*, volume 38, 1994.

The staff at Sage deserves thanks for making the entire production process as smooth and efficient as possible. Although there are no doubt countless individuals working behind the scenes, the people I have dealt with have been extremely helpful. They are: Carrie Mullen, Peter Labella, Renée Piernot, Druann Pagliossotti, Gillian Dickens, and Jennifer Morgan. Through their professionalism, these people have made this a fairly quick and fairly painless process.

Last, but certainly not least, I am grateful to my wife, Kathleen Dolan, who provided support on a number of different levels. Kathy saw and commented on more versions of this manuscript than anyone else. Her input included comments on everything from spelling and grammatical errors, to ideas about the structure of the book and suggestions about how to make the arguments clearer and more intelligible. Kathy was especially good at stopping me from adding more analysis when it really wasn't necessary. Because of this, the book is not only better, it's also done. In addition to academic input, Kathy also provided immeasurable support at home. Although I did not find writing this book to be a particularly arduous task, I did have to work a lot harder than I usually do, which did not make me a very happy person. Kathy put up with my "disposition" and did all that she could to make me comfortable. Those who know me well will understand what an onerous task this must have been. For this and everything else, I thank her.

Campaigns and Elections

Perhaps no political phenomenon captures the attention of the mass media and mass public in quite the same manner as an American presidential election campaign. During presidential election years, despite evidence of growing distrust of politicians, political parties, and candidates, the attention of the American public (perhaps, not by choice) is focused on campaign events from early summer through election day. Even for those who are not particularly interested in politics or the current race, it is difficult to avoid exposure to news about the campaign.

Despite all of the attention given to campaigns by the popular press, the academic community has expressed much less interest. Compared to other aspects of voting behavior and elections, students of electoral politics have paid scant attention to the dynamics of presidential campaigns and how campaigns influence public opinion.[1] At least part of the reason for this neglect is the widespread belief among students of elections that, if campaigns have any effect on the vote decision, it is minimal in comparison to other factors.

Essentially, most evidence from decades of voting behavior research suggests that voting behavior at the individual level is the product of long-term political attitudes and assessments of the incumbent presidential administration, and that election outcomes can be viewed as referenda on presidential performance. These perspectives on elections, which will be

1

explored later, do not leave much room for campaigns to play an important role. Nevertheless, there remains the fact that campaigns receive a lot of exposure and many interpretations of recent elections suggest that the campaigns—in some cases specific events in the campaigns—were important determinants of the eventual outcome.

Postelection Analyses

Following every election there is a virtual avalanche of postelection commentaries and analyses, sometimes academic in nature and sometimes not. A sampling of these analyses and commentaries from the last three elections summarizes quite nicely the competing views on the importance of campaigns to the electoral process.

CAMPAIGNS ARE IMPORTANT

The first perspective sees campaigns as playing a key role in determining voting behavior and election outcomes. Many adherents to this view of campaigns frequently cite specific campaign events or campaign strategies as being particularly important. For instance, following the 1988 campaign, Ed Rollins, a prominent Republican strategist, made the following comments when asked about the importance of the presidential debates during panel discussion on the campaign:

Ed Rollins: ". . . The truth of the matter is this campaign was over in four weeks."

David Gergen: "What four weeks?"

Ed Rollins: "The first four weeks of September. Once Bush got back up and went on the offensive, he put so many holes in the side of Michael Dukakis that it didn't matter if he won both debates." (Runkel 1989, 261)

In effect, Rollins is saying that the early aggressive strategy of the Bush campaign shattered any hope Dukakis might have had of winning. In other words, Bush won because of the campaign. Of course, it should not be surprising that Rollins, a campaign professional, would think that the conduct of the campaign destroyed Dukakis. This view is buttressed, however, by Abramson, Aldrich, and Rohde, who conclude in their analysis of the 1988 elections that, "regarding the outcome and voter choices, there are plenty of indicators that the campaign did matter" (1990, 52).

Journalistic analyses of campaigns also provide support for the importance of campaigns and, sometimes, single campaign events. The first chapter in Germond and Witcover's (1985) analysis of the 1984 campaign focuses on the importance of presidential debates. Germond and Witcover make the case that the Reagan campaign was seriously damaged by Reagan's weak performance in the first debate and by the questions about the president's age and ability to govern that followed the debate. According to Germond and Witcover, however, Reagan turned this around in the second debate when, in response to a question about his age, he responded that he would not exploit Mondale's youth and inexperience, a response that drew roars of laughter and applause from the audience. This response seemingly dispelled all concern about Reagan's age and changed the course of the campaign. According to Germond and Witcover, after Reagan delivered that line, "for all practical purposes, the presidential election was over" (1985, 9). Germond and Witcover (1989) similarly conclude, in a chapter called "The Killer Question," that the failure on the part of Dukakis, in the second presidential debate in 1988, to answer with any emotion Bernard Shaw's question about the death penalty—precisely, how he would feel about the death penalty if his wife, Kitty, were raped and murdered—contributed significantly to his defeat.

The argument that campaigns or campaign events affect vote choice and election outcomes has a great deal of natural appeal. After all, those of us who follow political campaigns can no doubt remember specific events—debate blunders or one-liners, campaign stunts such as Bush's tour of Boston Harbor or the Clinton/Gore bus tours, or political advertisements such as the Willie Horton ads or the Bear in the Woods ad—that certainly seemed to be important. Likewise, most partisans can, no doubt, recall some event that they thought at the time might significantly help or hurt their candidate. In short, campaigns provide a lot of interesting, high-profile moments that survive well after the campaign has ended. Imagining that anything we remember as being significant must have been so is, therefore, easy. But is it really that simple? Is the American electorate so fickle and open to persuasion? Needless to say, there are those who disagree.

CAMPAIGNS SERVE A LIMITED ROLE

Other analyses have found a more limited role for political campaigns, suggesting that they may have an effect on the election but one secondary to other influences. Light and Lake (1985), in their assessment of the 1984 election, recognize the futility of Mondale's efforts and attribute part of the reason for this to the Reagan campaign: "No matter how hard Mondale might have tried he could not have won the 1984 election without Reagan's help. But Reagan ran a masterful campaign" (1985, 83). Because the economy was growing and the president's popularity was on the rise, it would have been very difficult to unseat Reagan. The only way the campaign could have had a real influence would have been for the Reagan campaign to completely collapse. In effect, the prevailing conditions muted the potential for the campaign to have an influence. In a similar vein, Quirk and Dalager (1993) conclude that although there was clearly a difference in the effectiveness of the Bush and Clinton campaigns in 1992, the difference was not due to strategies or staff so much as to the conditions that the campaigns had to work with. As Quirk and Dalager put it, "Any Democratic organization in 1992 would have discovered the issues of change, the economy, and health care" (1993, 82). Pomper reached a similar conclusion about the 1988 campaign: "Campaigns can make a difference, and they did in 1988, but an analysis of the election results must begin with the recognition of structural conditions favorable to the Bush candidacy" (1989, 138).

This view of campaigns is echoed by Susan Estrich, one of Dukakis's chief strategists in the 1988 campaign. When asked about the effects of Reagan's rising popularity on the Bush/Dukakis race, Estrich said, " 'Maybe there were things we could have done right or better, but there wasn't a hell of a lot we could do about the lowest unemployment rate in twenty odd years and, how many, sixty sustained months of economic recovery' " (Runkel 1989, 260). Clearly, the Dukakis campaign felt limited by circumstances they could not control. This view of the efficacy of campaigns suggests that they may be relevant to the election but that other factors, usually the economy or presidential popularity, are probably more important and determine the degree to which campaigns can be effective.

CAMPAIGNS ARE NOT VERY RELEVANT

Finally, there are postelection analyses that suggest that campaigns are not very relevant at all. The best examples of this position can be found in analyses of the 1984 campaign. Pomper suggests that "for all the difference it made, America could have skipped the 1984 campaign. Whether the election had been held in the pre-primary winter, after the conventions, or in November's fall, Ronald Reagan would have won an overwhelming victory" (1985, 70). This position is echoed by Rosenstone, who concludes that "the important determinants of the 1984 presidential election were in place long before most people heard of Geraldine Ferraro, long before the candidates squared off in front of television cameras, and long before Americans met the bear in the woods (if there was a bear)" (1985, 25). At its extreme, this viewpoint argues that, barring something such as a total collapse on the part of one campaign, the campaigns have very little effect on the eventual outcome. For all of their sound and fury, campaigns are not very relevant to election outcomes. Instead, the macrocontext of the election matters the most.

Which of these perspectives is most accurate when applied to presidential campaigns in general? Is the manner in which candidates conduct their campaigns a critical factor in determining elections? Does the campaign have the potential to play an important role, depending on other factors? Or is the campaign largely irrelevant, providing little more than entertainment (at least for some of us)? These are the issues that are addressed in this book. In the remainder of this chapter, I will discuss reasons why we should expect campaigns to play a minor role in elections, as well as reasons why campaigns might play a more important role in determining voting behavior and election outcomes.

The Argument Against
Campaign Effects

Decades of voting behavior research suggest that campaigns should not be expected to play a consequential role in determining either voting behavior or election outcomes. Since the 1940s, volumes have been written on the determinants of American voting behavior. Although an exhaustive review of this literature is not practical (or necessary) in this chapter, the next two sections provide a description of the major streams of research on elections and illustrate how the dominant view of elections has evolved over time, paying special attention to the implications of this research for the role campaigns might play in presidential elections. For organizational purposes, the voting literature is broken into two different categories: studies that focus primarily on the behavior of individuals and studies that focus on explaining aggregate outcomes.

INDIVIDUAL-LEVEL EVIDENCE

In one of the earliest studies of mass voting behavior, Lazarsfeld, Berelson, and Gaudet (1944) tracked public opinion in Erie County, Ohio, during the 1940 election campaign. Although they began their study by focusing on how political predispositions (based on social groups) influence voting behavior, they also examined how things such as campaign propaganda, campaign events, and media coverage influence voting behavior. One innovative aspect of the Lazarsfeld et al. research effort was that they used a panel design in which the same individuals were surveyed at several points during the campaign. What they found was that most people expressed a vote intention in the spring, before the campaign, that coincided with their political predispositions, and voted according to those predispositions in the fall. Most important for the purposes of this analysis is their finding that very few people changed their expressed vote intention between May and October. In short, the campaign appeared to hold very little sway over how people voted. Instead, Lazarsfeld et al. concluded, campaigns tend to reinforce existing political preferences for those who already express a vote intention or activate latent predispositions among those who are undecided. *Conversion*—changing vote intention during the campaign—was found to be the least likely outcome (Lazarsfeld et al. 1944, 102-4).

Research that followed Lazarsfeld et al. focused on other determinants of voting behavior. In their seminal book, *The American Voter,* Campbell, Converse, Miller, and Stokes (1960) sought to go beyond the rather crude concept of political predispositions that was delineated in the earlier work of Lazarsfeld et al. Trying to account for the tendency of voters to support the same party in election after election, Campbell et al. developed the concept of party identification. *Party identification* is described as an affective orientation to the political parties that is held by most people and is a primary determinant of attitude formation and political behavior (Campbell et al. 1960, 121). Party identification is viewed as a long-term attitude that, though susceptible to change, is unlikely to change in response to short-term forces such as a political campaign (Campbell et al. 1960, 148-49). Party identification, as described by Campbell et al., not only influences vote choice but also attitudes toward candidates, issues, and political events.

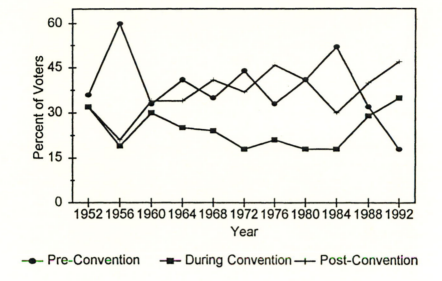

Figure 1.1. Time of Vote Decision, 1952-1992
SOURCE: American National Election Studies Cumulative Data File, 1952-1992 (ICPSR #8475).

Given the central role of party identification, it appeared unlikely that political campaigns could exercise much independent influence on voting behavior. According to *The American Voter,* people do not generally cast a vote based on the persuasiveness of campaign propaganda. Instead, their vote is heavily influenced by how they feel toward the parties—by their party identification.

Indeed, one of the important findings from *The American Voter* that bears directly on the importance of campaigns is that the vast majority of voters decide how to vote by the end of the party conventions, thereby rendering the fall campaign largely irrelevant to most voters. This finding from *The American Voter* has been generally supported over time. Although there is some variation from one election to the next, from 1952-1992 an average of 63% of all voters decided how to vote by the end of the nominating conventions (see Figure 1.1). According to Campbell et al., this confirms their idea that "the psychological forces guiding behavior arise before the campaign opens" (1960, 78).

Although the importance of partisanship has stood the test of time, there have been a number of critiques and new avenues of thought in the voting behavior literature. Perhaps the most important model developed since the publication of *The American Voter* is the referendum, or retrospective voting model. This model was initially developed by V. O. Key in his 1966 book, *The Responsible Electorate.* Although Key paid homage to the important role of party identification, his work was a clear departure. Key begins with an interesting premise: "Voters are not fools" (1966, 7). As a point of departure from previous literature, he rejects the notion that voters are "straitjacketed by social determinants or moved by unconscious urges triggered by devilishly skillful propagandists" (1966, 7). Key is clearest about the idea of retrospective voting when addressing the role of campaigns in the electoral process.

> The hullabaloo of a presidential campaign so commands our attention that we ascribe to campaigns great power to sway the multitude. Campaigning does change votes and it does bestir people to vote. *Yet other influences doubtless outweigh the campaign in the determination of the vote.* As voters mark their ballots they may have in their minds impressions of the last television spectacular of the campaign, but, *more important, they have in their minds recollections of their experiences of the past four years.*
>
> Events from the inauguration of an administration to the onset of the next presidential campaign may affect far more voters than the fireworks of the campaign itself. (1966, 9) [Italics added]

Key's language is strong and his conclusions are clear: Campaigns simply do not matter very much. What does matter is the performance of the incumbent administration and the interpretation of that performance by the voters. According to Key, voters compare their policy preferences with the policies of the incumbent party and then render a decision based on how satisfied they were with the performance of the party. In some ways, Key's findings are reminiscent of a Downsian (Downs, 1957) view of elections, with voters seeking to maximize their utility income by voting for the party closest to them on a policy continuum.

Unfortunately, Key died before the publication of *The Responsible Electorate,* so he was unable to continue research on retrospective voting. Others, however, attempted to sort out the relative influence of partisanship and policy preferences on vote choice. In the late 1970s, Page and Jones (1979) and Markus and Converse (1979) sought to disentangle the differential effects of party, candidates, and policy preferences on voting behavior. Although they reached somewhat different conclusions—Page and Jones assign more importance to policy evaluations whereas Markus and Converse see party identification as playing a more prominent role—neither of these analyses seemed to leave much room for influence from the campaign.

Key's ideas about retrospective voting were given more support by the work of Fiorina (1981). Fiorina provides a logical argument for the importance of retrospective evaluations that goes well beyond the work of Key. In the course of doing so, he provides a much more elaborate framework for the mechanism of retrospective voting than was found in Key. Fiorina is also clearer about what is expected of a retrospective voter. According to Fiorina, retrospective voters need not know the intricacies of policies either proposed or enacted by the parties; voters need know only whether they are satisfied with the outcomes or perceived outcomes of those policies. When Key discussed policy differences between the voters and the parties, it was not always in the same sense as the results-oriented retrospective voting described by Fiorina. Although many of the survey items examined by Key were results oriented, many of them were also means oriented, as we might expect to see in a Downsian model.

One of the strongest contributions of Fiorina's work is his integration of retrospective evaluations into a theory of party identification. Fiorina concedes the importance of party identification in the vote choice but argues that it is at least partially a function of a "running tally" of retrospective evaluations of the parties' performance. According to Fiorina, retrospective evaluations have both a direct and indirect (through party identification) effect on vote choice. Again, this perspective views elections as referenda on party performance, not as the consequence of a heated struggle between opposing groups of campaign strategists.

Much of the research that followed Fiorina (1981) focused on one aspect of government performance in particular: economic performance (Kinder, Adams, and Gronke 1989; Lewis-Beck 1988; Markus 1988). Although the evidence from these studies is mixed, one clear finding emerges: Assessments of the state of the economy and government performance in this area are very closely tied to support for the incumbent party.

One interesting yet infrequently cited contribution to this literature is Kiewiet and Rivers's analysis of popular support for Ronald Reagan (Kiewiet and Rivers 1985). Kiewiet and Rivers analyze support for Reagan during the 1984 campaign and find that changes in the unemployment rate were strongly related to changes in support for Reagan *during* the campaign. This finding, that changes in opinion during the campaign are related to noncampaign variables, suggests a less than omnipotent role for the campaign.

This body of individual-level research is not very supportive of the idea that campaigns play a pivotal role in shaping opinion and determining election outcomes. According to this literature, the voting decision largely is a product of long-standing predispositions (party identification) and retrospective evaluations of the performance of the parties. There is little room here for campaigns to change minds or influence behavior.

In all fairness, though, with the exception of Lazarsfeld et al. (1944), none of these studies have focused explicitly on the effects of political campaigns. Instead, it is usually inferred from other studies that because other variables, such as partisanship and retrospective evaluations, have such a strong effect on voting behavior, it is unlikely that campaigns have much influence. One recent study that directly addresses the effect of the campaign is Finkel's (1993) assessment of the "minimal effects" thesis. Finkel analyzes changes in public opinion during the campaign season, using a panel survey from the 1980 election. Finkel's findings are consistent with much of the earlier literature: Attitudes toward the candidates and parties are formed well before the campaign begins, and changes in these attitudes during the campaign, although having a statistically significant influence, are not very important determinants of vote choice, especially when compared to precampaign attitudes. Finkel concludes that for attitude changes during campaigns to have a nonminimal effect, they would have to be much larger in magnitude and much more lopsided than we have experienced in recent elections (1993, 19).

AGGREGATE EVIDENCE

Thus far, this discussion has focused primarily on studies that try to explain why individuals vote the way they do. A related branch of political science research, carried out at the aggregate level, has concentrated on trying to explain why elections turn out the way they do. Although they differ in terms of the level of analysis, the understanding of elections generated by these two approaches is essentially the same: Elections and voting behavior are heavily influenced by long-term political tendencies and by evaluations of the performance of the incumbent administration.

Because of the nature of this literature, it is useful to distinguish between what can be called statistical-explanation models and forecasting models. Statistical-explanation models try to account for statistical variation in the dependent variable—in this case, election outcomes—with independent variables that occur at roughly the same time as the dependent variable. A forecasting model, on the other hand, tries to "predict" election outcomes with independent variables that occur before the election is held. Lewis-Beck and Rice (1992) suggest that forecasting models should try to provide the most accurate forecast of the election outcome with the fewest possible variables as far before the election as possible.

Aggregate studies of election outcomes have demonstrated that election outcomes are easily explained by a few political and economic variables. Beginning with the important early work of Kramer (1971) and Tufte (1978), aggregate studies of elections, both presidential and congressional, have burgeoned into a virtual cottage industry. The early studies (Arcelus and Meltzer 1975; Bloom and Price 1975; Goodman and Kramer 1975; Kramer 1971; Li 1976; Tufte 1978) focused their energy on explaining statistical patterns in election results over time. Later studies (Abramowitz 1988; Campbell and Wink 1990; Fair 1978; Hibbs 1982; Lewis-Beck and Rice 1992) shifted the focus to predicting presidential election outcomes, producing highly accurate forecasting models.

Although most of the aggregate literature focused on national time series models, a number of other aggregate studies focused on explaining patterns of state-level presidential outcomes. Some of these are of the forecasting nature (Campbell 1992; Rosenstone 1983, 1985) whereas others are of the statistical explanation variety (Brunk and Gough 1983; Holbrook 1991).

Although there are a number of differences among these studies—some are forecasting models, others are not; some focus on the economy, others do not; some are time series, others are not—the vast majority of them have one thing in common: They find presidential election outcomes to be easily explained in terms of party strength in the electorate and retrospective evaluations of the incumbent party, as reflected in presidential popularity and objective mea-sures of economic performance. An important implication of these studies is that election outcomes are easily explained without considering any aspect of the campaign. This is particularly implied by the forecasting models, some of which provide accurate forecasts of elections based on data reflecting conditions before the campaign even begins. If elections can be accurately predicted in May, how is it possible for the campaign to have an effect?

Together, the individual-level and aggregate-level studies do not offer much encouragement for those who think campaigns are important. After reviewing these studies it certainly seems reasonable to ask ourselves why anyone would expect presidential campaigns to matter.

The Argument for Campaign Effects

Despite all evidence to the contrary, there are still some grounds for suggesting that campaigns do matter or at least have the potential to matter. The reasons for this optimism are (1) there are a significant number of people who decide how to vote during the campaign; (2) party identification is less important to the electorate today than it used to be; (3) there is significant fluctuation in candidate support during the campaign; and (4) as elections become more media oriented they generate a lot of information that can be used by voters as they consider how to vote.

TIMING OF THE VOTING DECISION

Earlier it was pointed out that one of the indicators of the irrelevance of the campaign is that most people decide how to vote before the campaign gets underway (see Figure 1.1). The fact that 63% of the electorate has already decided how they will vote by the end of the conventions was previously presented to suggest minimal campaign effects. The flip side of this, however, is that the remaining 37% constitute a significant portion of the electorate that, if mobilized by a campaign, can play an important role in the outcome. Another thing to consider is that the late deciders also happen to be those with weak party loyalties, individuals who are likely to be the most susceptible to campaign messages. From 1952-1992, 43% of all independents decided how to vote after the conventions, compared to 33% of all partisans.[2]

The way previous studies have defined early deciders may also stack the deck against expecting campaign effects. Those who decide how to vote after the nominating conventions are usually considered to be early deciders. One problem with this categorization is that it creates the impression that these people are not affected by the campaign. Given that the party conventions may be the most important events in the campaign, this assumption seems flawed. The data in Figure 1.1 illustrate that distinguishing the conventions from the rest of the campaign has real consequences for interpreting the potential effect of the campaign on voting behavior. From 1952-1992, between 18% and 35% of the electorate decided how they would vote during the party conventions. Given the prominence of the conventions, these people could be considered to have been influenced by the campaign. When these people are added to those who decided how to vote after the conventions, the number of people who decide how to vote during the campaign is much more impressive (mean = 61%).

Although this is true, it does not necessarily mean that the campaign determines vote choice. Recall that the early work of Lazarsfeld et al. (1944) and the later work of Finkel (1993) concluded that campaigns were only minimally effective because most people vote the way one would expect them to, based on their political predispositions. Lazarsfeld, Berelson, and Gaudet report that only 8% of their sample actually changed their preference during the 1940 campaign (Lazarsfeld et al. 1944, 102), and Finkel reports that only 4.8% changed their preference during the 1980 campaign (Finkel 1993, 15-16). However, although these numbers are small, they could be important in a close contest.

THE DECLINE OF PARTIES

Although partisanship generally remains a strong voting cue, our understanding of the nature of partisanship has undergone a significant transformation since the publication of *The American Voter*. Besides Fiorina's (1981) reformulation of party identification, one of the most significant changes has been the decline in the number of people who consider themselves partisans and the increase in the number who consider themselves independents. Figure 1.2 illustrates these changes over time. The percentage of the electorate identifying with a political party has declined from roughly 73% in the 1950s and 1960s to 61% by 1992. At the same time, the percentage identifying themselves as independents has increased from 22% in 1952 to 39% in 1992. Beyond the decline in self-identifying partisans, Wattenberg (1990) has documented a broader decline in support for the parties and a concomitant increase in candidate-centered politics in presidential campaigns (1991).

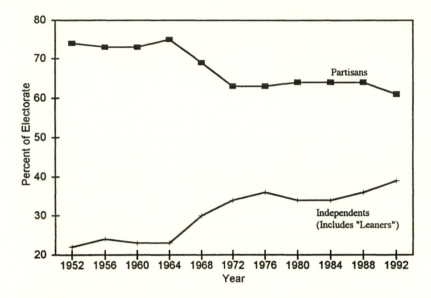

Figure 1.2. Changes in Partisanship, 1952-1992
SOURCE: American National Election Studies Cumulative Data File, 1952-1992 (ICPSR #5475).

As parties become a less relevant voting cue for more and more of the electorate, the vote decision should become more responsive to other variables. One possibility, of course, is that campaign rhetoric could take on more importance as partisanship wanes. Certainly, it is possible that other influences, such as retrospective evaluations, fill the void created by declining levels of partisanship. At any rate, it would appear that fewer voters are bound by partisan predispositions and may, therefore, be more susceptible to campaign messages.

FLUCTUATIONS IN OPINION
DURING THE CAMPAIGN

In a recent article on presidential campaigns, Gelman and King (1993) document fluctuations, sometimes very dramatic, in public support for candidates during the campaign season that apparently occur in response to campaign events. Both the 1988 and 1992 elections provide good examples of such fluctuation; in both years, the level of support for the candidates completely reversed itself from early summer to election day. In addition, Allsop and Weisberg (1988) and Weisberg and Allsop (1990) documented considerable variation in partisanship during the course of the 1984 campaign. Their analysis suggests that aggregate partisanship—usually thought of as a long-term attitude—changes in response to the influence of campaign events.

Of course, other, noncampaign events may be responsible for these changes. Indeed, Allsop and Weisberg list a number of noncampaign events, such as presidential travel and international incidents, that may have influenced changes in partisanship during the campaign season (1988, 1010). Also, recall that Kiewiet and Rivers (1985) found that changes in the unemployment rate were strongly related to changes in the level of support for presidential candidates during the campaign.

Although other influences may be at work, there can be little doubt that campaign events do influence public opinion. In particular, it has been demonstrated that the party conventions (Campbell, Cherry, and Wink 1992) and presidential debates (Geer 1988) sometimes influence candidate support. These campaign events receive almost undivided media attention when they occur and provide the candidates a forum for communicating to the voters. Of course there are other, lower-profile events—such as campaign photo opportunities, scandals, endorsements, and stump speeches—that may also influence public opinion. The important question is, how much opinion change does the campaign produce and how important is that change?

CAMPAIGN INFORMATION

The campaign is able to influence public opinion by performing its primary function: disseminating information. The campaign events just listed do not influence public opinion simply because they occur. Instead, they derive their influence from the amount and type of information they generate. In addition to media coverage of specific events, information is also provided through campaign advertisements. One way contemporary campaigns differ from forty years ago is that "television advertisements now represent the biggest expenditure of most campaigns" (West 1993, 7). Shively (1992) maintains that the ease with which campaign information can be obtained in the modern era has led to an important change in the structure of elections: Since 1960, there has been a growing tendency for electoral change from one election to the next to be the result of voter conversion rather than mobilization among partisans. Increased rates of voter conversion from one election to the next are certainly consistent with an increasingly important role for campaigns.

Popkin (1991) provides a thorough discussion of the role of information in political campaigns and makes a compelling argument for the importance of campaigns based on their information-generating nature. In Popkin's model of the "reasoning" voter, campaign information is vitally important.

> Campaigns make a difference because voters have limited information about government and uncertainty about the consequences of policies. If voters had full information and no uncertainty, they would not be open to influence from others, and hence there would be no campaigns. In reality, voters do not know very much about what government is doing or is capable of doing. Thus they are open to influence by campaigners who offer more information or better explanations of the ways in which government activities affect them. (Popkin 1991, 70)

Although Popkin's analysis focuses on presidential primaries, where one might expect information to be most important, his ideas are intended to apply to campaigns in general (Popkin 1991, 18).

Popkin is not alone in his argument about the importance of campaigns as agents of information. Salmore and Salmore (1989) argue that one of the results of the decline of partisanship is that parties are used less and less as a source of information about candidates. Instead, campaigns are replacing parties as a source of information about candidates (Salmore and Salmore 1989, 9). This theme is echoed in Wattenberg's thesis about the rise of candidate-centered campaigns (Wattenberg 1991). One cynical view holds that the information generated by campaigns is so important that the campaign consultants have the ability to easily manipulate candidate image and public opinion toward candidates (Hellinger and Judd 1991).

Clearly, the information generated by the campaigns does have the potential to play a role in shaping our view about the candidates. Jamieson points to the 1988 election as clear evidence that campaign messages influence public opinion, noting that "there can be little doubt that the Bush ads swayed perceptions of Dukakis" (1992, 484). Also, Bartels (1993) found that exposure to campaign information had an independent effect on changes in candidate evaluations during the 1980 campaign. If the campaign influences candidate perceptions, then it may ultimately influence vote choice. Even if changes in candidate evaluations do not affect vote choice, however, it could be said that the campaign has an effect—albeit a nonvoting effect—on political attitudes.

Gelman and King (1993) also assign importance to information, noting that voters learn about the campaign through the media, which report on campaign events, and then adjust their preferences accordingly. Through the information generated by campaigns and provided by the media, voters are able to form "enlightened" preferences (Gelman and King 1993, 433-435). Ansolabehere, Behr, and Iyengar (1993) also point to the importance of campaign information, noting that aggregate forecasting models are unable to account for changes in opinion during a campaign and that "fluctuations in polls show distinct patterns that can be linked to the pattern of campaign communication" (1993, 162).

How much campaign information matters in the end is not completely clear, however. Although Gelman and King (1993) make a strong case for the importance of information in helping voters decide for whom to vote, they also find that in the end this information helps voters decide to vote for the candidate we would expect them to vote for based on their political predispositions. This occurs because of the balanced nature of campaign information; if all candidates are waging serious campaigns, the information generated is likely to have a canceling-out effect (Gelman and King 1993, 449). If Gelman and King are correct, then campaigns are most likely to have a real effect on election outcomes when there exists an information asymmetry between the two campaigns, either because of biased reporting or because one campaign was run better than the other.

Who's Right?

What can we make of all of this? To be able to provide a definitive answer to the question of whether campaigns matter or not would be nice. Unfortunately, the evidence is not that clear. The opposing views laid out in this chapter present interesting possibilities. Clearly, partisan predispositions and retrospective evaluations appear to dominate the individual voting decision, and aggregate outcomes appear to be driven by evaluations of the performance of the incumbent party. On the other hand, it seems unwise, in the age of declining partisanship, media saturation, and high-tech campaign wizardry, to dismiss the effect of campaigns on public opinion and voting behavior.

Part of the problem with addressing the issue of whether campaigns matter lies in defining what it means to "matter." All too often, it is assumed that for campaigns to be relevant they have to determine the election outcome. If what we mean by "matter" is more broadly construed, however, it is easier to find evidence of significant campaign effects. Indeed, some of the evidence against campaign effects can be used to support assertions of a demonstrable effect from the campaign. The panel studies of Lazarsfeld et al. (1944) and Finkel (1993) found that a small percentage of the population (8% in 1940 and 4.8% in 1980) actually change their mind during a campaign. These "converted" voters may represent a small percentage of the voting public but they also represent an artifact of the campaign. According to both Lazarsfeld et al. and Finkel, the more likely effect of the campaign is to reinforce or activate latent partisan predispositions. Typically, the small rates of conversion and the reinforcement and activation functions of the campaign are used to illustrate the inefficacy of presidential campaigns. One could argue, however, that activation and reinforcement are very important parts of the voting decision and that even small rates of conversion can be important. To the degree that these phenomena can be attributed to the campaign, they point to the importance of campaigns.

One need look no further than the 1992 election for additional evidence of the effect of campaigns. Ross Perot's candidacy was a very important part of the campaign and, although it may not have had an effect on who won the race, his 19% of the vote clearly changed the nature of the outcome. One could argue that Clinton would have won with or without Perot in the race, but Perot's candidacy in all likelihood robbed Clinton of a majority victory (more on this in Chapter 6). The point here is that there are many ways other than determining election outcomes that a campaign can "matter."

Inevitably, however, the importance of campaigns tends to be judged in terms of their effect on election outcomes. Given what we know about the importance of other variables in the voting calculus, this may be an unrealistic criterion to apply to presidential campaigns. On the other hand, it does not seem unreasonable to expect that campaigns should be able to move public opinion and contribute to the outcome; after all, this is their primary goal.

Most of this book focuses on how campaigns influence voting behavior and election outcomes. Given what seems to be the determinative effect of noncampaign factors on election outcomes, this focus establishes a very tough test for campaign effects. Nevertheless, as the arguments unfold, it will become clear that campaigns do influence candidate support and that this influence can be strong enough to alter election outcomes.

The Plan of This Book

In this book, the issue of campaign effects is approached from a number of different angles. One question to be addressed is the extent to which presidential campaigns influence the actual election outcome. This is an aggregate question and is addressed using aggregate data. A related question is how much influence campaigns have on changes in public opinion during the campaign. This, too, is an aggregate question that is primarily addressed with aggregate data. Finally, this book examines the effects of campaigns on individual-level public opinion and voting behavior. To the extent possible, this issue is addressed with data from national public opinion surveys.

Although other campaigns are discussed and, to some extent, analyzed, most of the analysis in this book focuses on the presidential elections of 1984, 1988, and 1992. These elections are given more attention for several reasons. First, they are contemporary and therefore represent the state of modern campaigns. Second, much of data used in the analysis are not available for earlier elections, thus precluding a more thorough analysis of previous elections. Third, these elections represent a nice mix of different electoral environments: In 1984, the sitting incumbent was relatively popular, presided over a growing economy, and went on to a landslide victory; in 1988, the sitting vice president won the election under generally favorable conditions, although by a less impressive margin than his predecessor; and in 1992, the sitting president appeared to be brought down by a stagnant economy and sinking approval ratings. Also, recall from the early part of this chapter that some saw the 1984 election as a case in which the campaigns were virtually irrelevant and the 1988 and 1992 elections as cases in which the campaigns had a significant, if not determinative, effect. Again, although much of the analysis will focus on campaigns from 1984 to 1992, data from all campaigns from 1952-1992 will contribute to this book.

In the next chapter (Chapter 2) the arguments against campaign effects are analyzed in greater detail using both aggregate and individual-level evidence. The next section of the book focuses on arguments in favor of strong campaign effects.

In Chapter 3, a model of campaign effects is developed and several hypotheses concerning the role of campaign events and national conditions are presented. This chapter includes an expanded discussion of the important role of information in the campaign process. Chapter 4 examines the effect of the party nominating conventions on public opinion during the campaign. Chapter 5 follows suit and analyzes the effect of presidential debates on candidate support at both the aggregate and individual level. Chapter 6 is the last chapter of analysis and integrates conventions, debates, other types of campaign events, and national conditions into a single model of candidate support during and across campaigns. The final chapter (Chapter 7) summarizes the findings from the previous six chapters and offers some general conclusions concerning the role of campaigns in presidential elections.

Notes

1. This of course applies to general election campaigns. There have been a number of important studies of the dynamics of presidential primary campaigns (Aldrich 1980; Bartels 1988).

2. These data were derived from the National Election Studies, 1952-1992.

Evidence Against Campaign Effects

The strongest arguments against finding significant campaign effects lie not in the existing scholarship on campaigns but in the body of scholarship pointing to other variables, at both the aggregate and individual levels, as the primary determinants of voting behavior and election outcomes. In short, this evidence suggests that election outcomes are too easily predicted without considering campaign variables and that voting behavior is too heavily influenced by long-term predispositions and attitudes toward presidential performance for campaigns to have any meaningful effect. Although findings of this nature do not rule out the possibility of significant campaign effects, they certainly are consistent with a more pessimistic view of the role of campaigns. Before beginning a detailed analysis of campaign variables, it is useful to examine the strength of competing explanations of voting behavior and election outcomes. This chapter provides an examination of these arguments at both the aggregate and individual levels.

Aggregate Models

In 1992, Bill Clinton defeated the incumbent president, George Bush, taking 43% of the vote to Bush's 37%. One interpretation of this outcome is that Clinton ran a good campaign and Bush did not. After all, it seemed that the Bush campaign never did get going and had difficulty articulating a clear message, at least one that resonated well with the American public. The Clinton team, on the other hand, seemed to have run an almost flawless campaign. They campaigned hard, emphasized the message of change, and provided quick responses to accusations made by the other side. In many ways, to the casual observer, it may seem clear that the campaign had a lot to do with the outcome in 1992.

Another way of looking at the 1992 election, however, suggests that the Republicans lost the election despite a golden opportunity handed to them by the Democrats in the form of candidate Clinton. Candidates are certainly a major part of the campaign and in some ways Clinton may have been the most vulnerable candidate the Democrats could present: He was a little-known governor from a state with many problems; he was publicly accused of marital infidelity; there were important questions about the methods he used to avoid the draft; he admitted having smoked marijuana (but not inhaling); and his reputation for waffling on issues contributed to feelings of mistrust. How could Bush lose against a candidate like this? But candidate characteristics do not tell the entire story of the election. Perhaps a better question is whether there was any way George Bush could have won in 1992.

In October 1992, only 34% of the public approved of the job George Bush was doing as president, and an overwhelming majority (68%) felt that the economy had gotten worse during the past year.[1] With a political and economic climate of this nature, it could be that the best of campaigns would have fallen short for the Republicans in 1992. In fact, it could be that the Republicans waged the best campaign possible. The same logic can be applied to previous elections. How could the Democrats have won any of the elections in the 1980s? Certainly, in 1980, President Carter's anemic popularity rating, coupled with the economic situation and foreign affairs problems, presented a daunting prospect for the Democrats regardless of campaign strategy. In 1984, the Democrats faced a popular Republican president and a growing economy, and in 1988, Reagan was still popular and confidence in the economy was high. Would better-run Democratic campaigns have made a difference in any of these years? From the point of view of aggregate forecasting models, the answer to this question is that, to the extent that accurate forecasts based on variables such as the economy and presidential popularity can be made, campaigns exert little net influence on election outcomes.

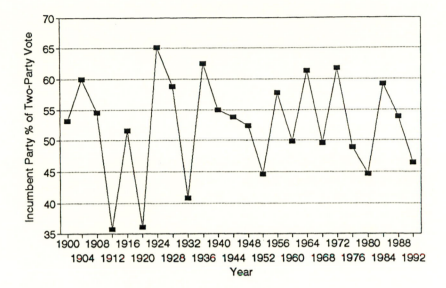

Figure 2.1. Presidential Election Outcomes, 1900-1992

How predictable are election outcomes? In this chapter, both a long view and a shorter view of the predictability of elections are provided. First, a model of presidential elections in the twentieth century is presented. This model is not a strict forecasting model but a statistical explanation model, as described in Chapter 1. This is followed by a true forecasting model of election outcomes from 1952 to 1992.

TWENTIETH-CENTURY PRESIDENTIAL ELECTIONS

The first test of the efficacy of aggregate models focuses on twentieth-century presidential elections. Figure 2.1 illustrates the variation in presidential election outcomes in the 1900s; the horizontal axis represents the year of the election and the vertical axis represents the percentage of the two-party (Democrat and Republican) vote going to the incumbent presidential party. One thing these data clearly illustrate is that there is a lot of variation in presidential election outcomes. This is especially true in the early period, where there are wide swings in support from one election to the next. The key question for this analysis is whether this variation is predictable based on noncampaign variables, or if it is due to other influences, perhaps varying campaign techniques.

Focusing on economic growth provides some indication of the degree to which these outcomes follow predictable patterns. The four elections in which the incumbent party was able to garner over 60% of the two-party vote (1924, 1936, 1964, and 1972) were all years of relatively strong economic growth: The average increase in gross national product, at constant prices, was 6.94% (this is somewhat inflated by the 14% growth rate in 1936).[2] Looking at those elections in which the incumbent party fared most poorly provides mixed evidence for the predictability of elections. In three of the five elections in which the incumbent party received less than 45% of the two-party vote, the economy actually shrank during the election year. The two exceptions to this are 1912 and 1952, years in which the economy grew at respectable rates, 4.7% and 3.9%, respectively.

Why did the incumbent party fail to hold onto the White House in 1912 and 1952, even though the economy was quite strong in both years? The election of 1912 represents a truly unusual circumstance in American politics. The Republicans held the White House under William Howard Taft. Taft, however, was challenged in the primaries by former Republican president Theodore Roosevelt. Roosevelt actually beat Taft in the primaries but Taft's forces controlled the convention and Taft was able to secure the nomination (*Congressional Quarterly* 1987). Roosevelt went on to run as the candidate for the Progressive party, a major third-party movement in the early twentieth century, and managed to finish ahead of Taft on election day; the Democratic candidate Woodrow Wilson carried the day, however. Given the unusual circumstances of this election—two candidates running who had served as Republican presidents—it is little wonder that the outcome is a deviation from what could be expected based on economic growth. The election of 1952 is a little harder to explain away, although three factors seem to provide likely explanations. First, the Democrats had held the White House since 1932. According to Alan Abramowitz (1988), the longer a party holds the White House the harder it becomes to keep it, perhaps because it is easier to convince voters that it is time for a change. Second, the Republican candidate Dwight Eisenhower was a war hero held in high esteem by the American people. Third, the Korean War was not going well and the blame for this rested with the incumbent party. The combination of these factors may have been enough to convince voters that it was time to give the Republicans a chance regardless of the economic circumstances.

One danger inherent in these types of explanations is that each election has its own unique set of candidates and circumstances that might be able to "explain" the election outcome. The issue at hand is whether election outcomes can be generally explained by factors that do not refer to the specific and unique circumstances of the election. Trying to develop a model to explain the 24 elections from 1900 to 1992 is a daunting task. Elections today are so different from elections in the early part of the century (consider the changes in the role of the mass media, along with term limits on presidents) that one might reasonably suggest that a single model should not be applied to the entire era. To the extent that this is true, the pattern of outcomes presented in Figure 2.1 presents a strong test for the predictability of elections.

A Model of Twentieth-Century Presidential Elections

In this section, a model of presidential elections is developed and tested for all elections since 1900, with the exception of the election of 1912, which is excluded due to the unusual circumstances described earlier. The dependent variable in this analysis is the percentage of the two-party popular vote won by the incumbent presidential party. The model described here is intended to illustrate the degree to which the wide swings in presidential vote depicted in Figure 2.1 follow a predictable pattern.

One element that both forecasting and nonforecasting aggregate election models include is a measure of economic performance (see Kramer 1971; Lewis-Beck and Rice 1992; Tufte 1978). Measures of economic performance allow the incorporation of a referendum component to election cycles. In good economic times voters are expected to be willing to return the party in power and in bad economic times voters are expected to be more willing to change the party in power. In this analysis, the percentage change in gross national product (at constant prices) during the election year is used as a measure of the state of the economy. This is a broad measure of economic vitality and should serve as a good overall indicator of the state of the economy.

In addition to the referendum component, a measure of partisan strength is also included. At different times throughout this century, popular support for the parties has experienced significant ebbs and flows. In the absence of a survey-based measure, such as party identification, a surrogate measure of party support is used. Specifically, the strength of the incumbent presidential party in Congress is used as a measure of party strength in the electorate.

This is measured as the percentage of seats held by the president's party in the House of Representatives in the two-year period before the election. Although this may not be an ideal measure of party support, it should serve as a reliable indicator of any shifts in the political winds since the last election that might affect presidential elections.

In addition to the state of the economy and party strength, two other variables are added to the analysis. The first is a control variable for whether or not the incumbent president is seeking reelection. This control is included not just because the office of the presidency can bring significant resources to bear on the presidential race but also because incumbent presidents may choose to run for reelection when conditions are most favorable to them (of course, reelection bids have been limited since the 22nd Amendment was adopted in 1951). In addition, another variable is added to control for the party of the presidency. This variable is needed to take into account the possibility that one party may hold a long-term advantage over the other in presidential contests. Specifically, due to the bifurcated nature of the American party system it might be expected that the Republicans hold an advantage in presidential elections. The basis for this expectation is found in the cleavage between the Northern and Southern wings of the Democratic party. Although southern Democrats have been able to elect conservative Democrats at the state and local level, the national party has offered very few presidential candidates with widespread appeal to the conservative preferences of southern voters. As a result, it has been relatively easy, especially in the postwar era, for Republican presidential candidates to attract southern Democratic votes. A preliminary look at the data supports the idea of a Republican advantage. Since 1900, the Republicans have won fourteen elections to the Democrats' nine (the election of 1912 is not included due to the unusual circumstances described earlier), and the Republicans have averaged 52.1% of the two-party vote to the Democrats' 47.9%.

The ordinary least squares (OLS) regression analysis of the model is presented in Table 2.1. The results of the analysis suggest that presidential elections do follow a generally predictable pattern and that most of the variables in the model influence presidential election in the anticipated manner. The coefficient for change in the gross national product (GNP) indicates that for every percentage point increase in GNP during the election year the president's party receives an additional .82 percentage points of the two-party vote. Party strength in the electorate is also an important influence on presidential elections. The president's party receives an additional .40%

Table 2.1   A Model of Twentieth-Century Presidential Elections
(OLS Estimates)

Variable	b	SE	t-Score
Constant	10.37	9.35	1.11
Percentage of GNP growth	.82	.20	4.06**
Party strength in Congress	.40	.13	3.10**
Party (1 = Dem, 2 = Rep)	11.93	2.68	4.45**
Incumbency	2.52	2.53	1.11

$N = 23$; $R^2 = .65$; Adj. $R^2 = .57$; Mean absolute error = 3.56; $\rho = -.03$ (n.s.).
**$p < .05$ (two-tailed).

of the two-party presidential vote for every percentage point of congressional seats it holds prior to the election. The coefficient for party of the president indicates that Republicans hold a sizable advantage of 11.9 percentage points in presidential elections, all else held equal. The only variable that does not demonstrate a significant effect is incumbency, the coefficient for which is in the anticipated direction but not statistically significant.

Beyond the direction and significance of coefficients, measures of the overall fit of the regression model provide a description of how well the model explains presidential elections. According to the adjusted R^2 statistic the model explains 57% of the variance in election outcomes from 1900 to 1992. One interpretation of this statistic is that the error in predicting election results is reduced by 57% when the values of the independent variables are taken into account.[3] A more direct measure of accuracy, however, is the mean absolute error (MAE) of the estimate, which tells how far off the regression estimates are, on average, from the actual vote. The MAE in Table 2.1 is 3.56, indicating that, on average, the regression estimates were within 3.56 percentage points of the actual election result.

Although both the R^2 and the MAE suggest a good fit between the model and the data, a clearer representation of how well the model fits is given in Figure 2.2, which plots the predicted and actual vote percentages from 1900 to 1992. The predicted and actual values follow the same pattern throughout the time period but some years are clearly better predicted than others. In four elections (1940, 1956, 1960, and 1988) the estimated results were within less than 1 percentage point of the actual result, whereas in four elections (1900, 1948, 1964, and 1992) the predicted results were more than 6 percentage points off the actual results. Cynics will note that in four cases (highlighted with a rectangle in Figure 2.2) the model estimates the wrong winner.

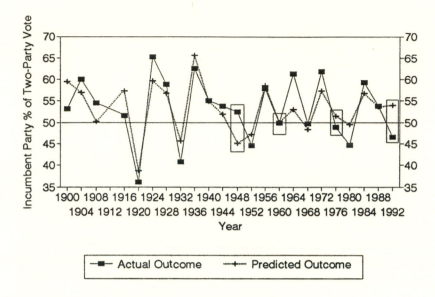

Figure 2.2. Predicted and Actual Election Outcomes

Although there is a close correspondence between the predicted and actual outcomes presented in Figure 2.2, there is enough error in the model to suggest that the relationship between election outcomes and aggregate conditions is not as deterministic as it might seem. For instance, how could an aggregate model predict, as this model does, that George Bush would win in 1992? The answer is threefold. First, this model is intended to demonstrate a general relationship between noncampaign variables and election outcomes—it is not intended to provide highly accurate forecasts. In general, the data do follow a predictable pattern, although some cases are explained better than others. Second, the data analyzed here cover a vast period of time during which the environment of presidential elections has changed remarkably. One could argue that comparing elections from the last three decades to those in the early part of the century is similar to comparing apples to oranges. Given this, the results in Table 2.1 are even more impressive. Third, because the analysis covers such a long period of time, many important pieces of information, such as survey-based measures of presidential popularity, are not available for most years and could not be included in the analysis. The inclusion of this type of information could prove to be very useful.

FORECASTING ELECTIONS IN THE MODERN ERA

All three of the problems that plagued the analysis in Table 2.1 can be overcome if the focus is shifted to elections in a more contemporary era. In this section, a forecasting model is developed and applied to presidential elections from 1952 to 1992. As with the earlier analysis, the dependent variable in the forecasting model is the percentage of the two-party presidential vote received by the incumbent presidential party.

Recall from the discussion of forecasting models in Chapter 1 that the goal of a forecasting model is to provide as accurate a forecast of the election as possible with as few variables as necessary as far before the election as possible. With this in mind, two criteria were used to select the variables to be included in the model. First, the variables had to be measurable in time well before the election occurred. If the variables do not occur, or cannot be measured before the election, then the model is not capable of forecasting a result. Second, the variables have to be exogenous from the general election campaign. If the model is intended to reflect the effect of noncampaign variables, any variables that reflect the effect of the campaign should be excluded. This means not only that campaign variables must be excluded but that the independent variables must occur before the general election campaign gets into full swing.

Given these criteria, the forecasting model used here is based on the model developed by Alan Abramowitz (1988), with some significant differences. The Abramowitz model includes a measure for presidential popularity, for change in GNP, and for measuring how long the incumbent party has held the presidency. This last variable is included as a "time for a change" control. The logic behind this variable is that if the party in power has held the White House for at least two terms, it should be easier to convince the public that it is time for a change (Abramowitz 1988, 844).

Although the Abramowitz model is used as a framework, the model developed here departs somewhat from Abramowitz's model. Specifically, the independent variables are presidential approval in the second quarter of the election year, the aggregate level of satisfaction with change in personal finances in May of the election year, and a dummy variable indicating whether the incumbent party has held the White House for at least two terms.[4] The economic indicator, change in personal finances, is based on a survey question that asks respondents how they are doing financially compared to a year ago. The exact measure used here is the relative index of "better" responses to "worse" responses; high values indicate greater satisfaction

Table 2.2 .   A Forecasting Model for Presidential Elections, 1952-1992

Variable	b	SE	t-Score
Constant	18.416	3.849	4.78**
Popularity	.096	.049	1.94*
Aggregate personal finances	.294	.0442	6.66**
Party tenure	−4.533	1.0270	−4.41**

$N = 11$; $R^2 = .97$; Adj. $R^2 = .95$; Mean absolute error = .81; $\rho = .003$ (n.s.).
*$p < .10$ (two-tailed); **$p < .05$ (two-tailed).

with change in personal finances. This measure is used instead of change in GNP for two reasons. First, as Abramowitz points out, reliable estimates of growth in GNP are usually not available until after the election has taken place, thereby making it difficult to forecast an election result before it actually occurs. Second, change in personal finances is a survey-based measure of economic vitality and, hence, reflects the perceptions of the mass public. In all likelihood, the objective state of the economy does not affect election outcomes so much as the public's perception of the state of the economy. The measure used here should serve as a good indicator of the underlying sense of economic security prior to the start of the general election campaign. One drawback to using the survey-based measure, however, is that it limits the analysis to the years from 1952 to 1992 because May surveys were not taken on a regular basis until 1951.

The results of the forecasting analysis are presented in Table 2.2. These findings provide strong support for the forecasting model. All variables are statistically significant and in the anticipated direction.[5] The incumbent presidential party benefits from high levels of presidential popularity and relatively positive evaluations of personal finances. On the other hand, the longer the incumbent party has held office the harder it is to maintain that hold. More telling from a forecasting point of view is the accuracy of the model. The adjusted R^2 for the model is .95, indicating a 95% reduction in error due to the variables in the model. The mean absolute error of the predictions is equally impressive: On average, the predicted outcome was less than 1 percentage point (.81) off the actual outcome.

The accuracy of these predictions is more clearly presented in Figure 2.3, which plots the actual results and the forecast results for each of the elections. The vertical distance between actual and forecast values represents the level of error in the estimate. The largest error (2.59 percentage points) occurred

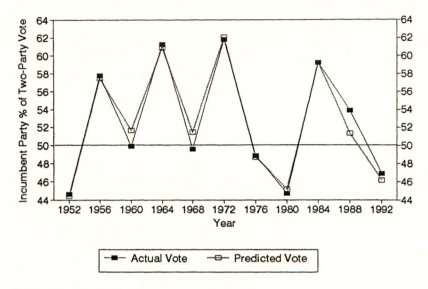

Figure 2.3. Accuracy of Forecasts, 1952-1992

in 1988, and the smallest error (–.01 percentage points) occurred in 1984. Note that in many cases the predicted value is so close to the actual value that the symbols virtually overlap. In two years (1960 and 1968), however, the model predicts the wrong winner. Given how close these elections were (Kennedy won in 1960 by a margin of .2 percentage points, and Nixon won in 1968 by a margin of .7 percentage points), it is not surprising that even an extremely accurate forecasting model would predict incorrect outcomes. Even in these two years, the forecast was less than 2 percentage points off the actual outcomes.

One possible interpretation of these results is that the difference between the actual outcomes and the forecast outcomes represents the effects of unspecified variables, possibly the effects of the campaign.[6] Because the forecasts are based on data from a period before the general election gets into full swing, the error in the estimates could be due to the intervening general election campaign. If this is accepted as a real possibility, the net effects of the presidential campaigns range from –.01 percentage points in 1984 to 2.59 percentage points in 1988—not very impressive. Of course, another possibility is that the error in the model is due to other, unspecified noncampaign factors.

Table 2.3   A Fall Forecasting Model for Presidential Elections, 1952-1992

Variable	b	SE	t-Score
Constant	22.351	7.693	2.91**
Popularity	.248	.106	2.33**
Aggregate personal finances	.178	.093	1.90*
Party tenure	−3.594	2.079	−1.73

$N = 11$; $R^2 = .89$; Adj. $R^2 = .84$; Mean absolute error = 1.74; $\rho = .41$ (n.s.).
*$p < .10$ (two-tailed); **$p < .05$ (two-tailed).

A Fall Model

The reason for using independent variables measured in the spring of the election year is to try to protect against their values being influenced by campaign activities. Values of presidential popularity and perceptions of personal finances in the fall of an election year are possibly endogenous to campaign activity. In other words, the campaign itself could influence presidential approval and economic perceptions. If this were the case, then an aggregate model based on data collected during the fall of an election year could reflect both noncampaign and campaign effects. This raises an interesting question: How does the forecasting model in Table 2.2 measure up when compared to a forecasting model based on variables measured in the fall of the election year? If a model based on measures taken before the general election campaign begins can provide estimates as accurate as those generated from a model based on measures taken close to election day, then it would appear that campaign effects are truly minimal. To make this comparison, the forecasting model is estimated again using presidential popularity from the closest month prior to the election in which the Gallup organization asked the approval question and perceived change in personal finances in November of the election year.

The results of this analysis, shown in Table 2.3, indicate a poorer fit between the actual election results and estimates based on measures taken more proximate to the election than between the actual results and estimates based on measures taken in the spring of election year. The adjusted R^2 (.84), although still impressive, is considerably smaller than that obtained by the spring model. Moreover, the mean absolute error of the fall model (1.74) is more than twice the size of the mean absolute error of the spring model (.81). On the positive side, the fall model predicted the correct winner for the 1968 election, which the spring model predicted incorrectly. Still, on average, the estimates generated by the spring model are far more accurate than those generated by the fall model. Presidential popularity and personal finances are still significant and positive influences but length of tenure no longer has a significant effect.

These findings are quite interesting. Apparently, the most accurate forecasts are made in the spring of the election year. Forecasts based on measures taken in the fall that may in part reflect the influence of the campaign are much less accurate. One possible explanation for this finding is that the intensity of the campaign activity in the fall may politicize evaluations of presidential performance and economic activity in such a way that these variables are more likely to reflect short-term influences of the campaign in the fall than in the spring. To the extent that the fall indicators pick up the effect of the campaign, they may be less likely to reflect the true underlying levels of satisfaction with the current administration and the state of the economy. When answering survey questions about presidential approval and economic assessments in the fall, voters may mimic the political rhetoric of the campaign rather than express their true, more deeply seated feelings. When acting in the voting booth, however, it is possible that voters express their "actual" evaluations rather than those reflecting the campaign rhetoric. Still, it could be that the fall model also does a good job of explaining election outcomes—just not as good as the spring model.

Individual-Level Evidence

The evidence previously presented illustrates the predictability of presidential election outcomes in the aggregate electorate. But what about individual-level voting behavior? Does it also follow a regular, predictable pattern? If individual-level voting behavior follows a predictable path, what are the implications for campaign effects? To the extent that individual-level voting behavior is driven by the same set of noncampaign variables from one election to the next, there is even more evidence of minimal opportunities for the campaign to influence voting behavior.

One of the problems with studying campaign effects at the individual level is that most public opinion surveys are not designed with this purpose in mind. The main data source used by students of elections, the biennial National Election Study (NES), is primarily designed to study the effect of partisanship, issues, and personalities on voting behavior. The primary drawback to the NES is that it lacks a dynamic component that would allow for a clear analysis of how campaign events produce changes in political attitudes.[7] In addition, the NES includes very few survey items that are specifically intended to capture the effects of political campaigns. Given this, one can make inferences only about the possible effects of campaign variables based on the ability of a cross-sectional model to explain variation in voting behavior.

A MODEL OF INDIVIDUAL-LEVEL VOTING

Two schools of thought dominate the field of voting studies. The first, originating with *The American Voter,* suggests that voting is the product of long-term political predispositions and personal background characteristics. The second, retrospective voting, established by Key (1966) and Fiorina (1981), downplays the importance of long-term forces and suggests that elections are essentially referenda on the performance of the incumbent presidential party. These two schools of thought are by no means mutually exclusive and are frequently integrated into a single model of voting behavior, as will be done in the model tested here. The model is not intended to be a perfect representation of voting behavior. Instead, the purpose of the model is to illustrate that it is possible to explain a significant share of voting behavior with a few core variables representing the traditional schools of thought.

The dependent variable in this model is vote choice, measured with a dichotomous dependent variable scored 1 for those who voted for the incumbent party candidate and scored 0 for those who voted for some other candidate. The long-term independent variables used in this model can be broken down into two categories: attitudinal and demographic variables. The long-term attitudinal variables are party identification and political ideology. Specifically, dummy variables are included that identify the respondent as Democrat or Republican and liberal or conservative (see Table 2.4 for a complete description of all variables). Dichotomous variables are also included to capture the effects of a number of demographic characteristics: union membership, race, urban residency, and residency in the South. Democrats, liberals, African Americans, people from union households, non-Southerners, and city residents are expected to support Democratic candidates. Republicans, conservatives, those from nonunion house-

Table 2.4   Variables Included in Individual-Level Voting Model

Vote choice	1 = Incumbent party candidate, 0 = Other (v705)
Democrat	1 = Weak or strong Democratic identifier, 0 = Other (v301)
Republican	1 = Weak or strong Republican identifier, 0 = Other (v301)
Liberal	1 = Liberal or extremely liberal, 0 = Other (v803)
Conservative	1 = Conservative or very conservative, 0 = Other (v803)
City	1 = Central city resident, 0 = Other (v111)
Race	1 = Black, 0 = Other (v106)
South	1 = Resident of one of sixteen deep South or border states, 0 = Other (v113)
Union	1 = Union household, 0 = Nonunion household (v127)
Approval	1 = Approve of the way the president is handling his job, 0 = Disapprove (v450)

NOTE: All variables are taken from the American National Election Studies Cumulative Data File (ICPSR #8475); the variable number is indicated in parentheses.

holds, Southerners, and nonurban dwellers are expected to support Republican candidates.

Retrospective evaluations are captured with a single variable: the degree to which the respondent approves of the job the president is doing. Other variables, such as evaluations of the state of the economy and satisfaction with personal finances, were not included because they were not all available for every year and, with presidential approval in the equation, they rarely had a significant effect on vote choice. Of course, those who approve of the way the president is handling his job are expected to be more likely to support the incumbent party than those who do not approve.

Variable selection for the model was driven by two concerns: focusing on a few core variables that could provide an adequate theoretical and empirical explanation of vote choice, and selecting variables that were available for as many elections as possible. This last criterion limits the analysis to presidential elections from 1972 to 1992 because the NES did not adopt the presidential approval and political ideology questions until 1972.

The analysis of the voting model, presented in Table 2.5, supports the position that voting behavior is a function of long-term political attitudes and retrospective evaluations of the performance of the incumbent administration. Party identification has a significant effect in the anticipated direction in each of the six election years. Political ideology has a less consistent but still generally important effect on vote choice; eight of the twelve ideology coefficients are significant (less than .05) and in the anticipated direction. Presidential approval has a significant effect in the anticipated direction and is also the most influential variable in each of the years (because all variables

Table 2.5   Analysis of Individual-Level Voting Behavior, 1972-1992
(Logistic Regression)

	1972	*1976*	*1980*	*1984*	*1988*	*1992*
Constant	.917***	−1.805***	−2.376***	−1.488***	−1.637***	−2.216***
Democrat	−1.094***	−1.357***	1.320***	−1.705***	−1.434***	−1.281***
Republican	2.386***	1.031***	−1.484***	1.188***	1.782***	.949***
Liberal	−1.841***	−.082	.995***	−.669*	−1.520***	−1.274***
Conservative	.813	.995***	−.598*	.827**	.995***	1.079***
Race	−2.341***	−1.140***	2.059***	−1.441***	−2.089***	−1.079***
Union	−.065	−.231	.625**	−.461*	−.349	.069
City	−.258	.859	.327	−.511*	−.188	.321
South	.795***	.145	.168	.250	.493*	.535***
Approval	2.683***	2.924***	2.439***	3.709***	2.630***	2.360***
% Correct	87.3	83.6	84.5	89.8	86.0	84.9
PRE	.618	.638	.547	.749	.692	.572
Model chi-square	362.9	690.3	390.4	856.9	688.6	773.3
N	558	916	653	1,030	916	1,311

*$p < .10$ (two-tailed); **$p < .05$ (two-tailed); ***$p < .01$ (two-tailed).

are dichotomous, the relative magnitude of their effects can be assessed by comparing the size of the coefficients).

The results are less consistent for the sociodemographic variables. The most consistent result for this group of variables is from the coefficients for race, which is significant and in the anticipated direction (African Americans less likely to vote Republican) in each of the years. None of the other sociodemographic variables demonstrate a consistently significant effect, although each variable is significant in at least one of the years.

In addition to the significance of the individual coefficients, the overall model does a good job of explaining vote choice. The model is able to cor rectly predict vote choice for the vast majority of voters, ranging from 83.6% predicted correctly in 1976 to 89.8% predicted correctly in 1984. The proportional reduction in error (PRE) statistics are also impressive. This statistic tells how much the model reduces prediction error, compared to simply guessing the modal category of the dependent variable. The range in PRE is from a 54.7% reduction in error in 1980 to a 74.9% reduction in error in 1984. All in all, the model does a very good job of accounting for vote choice.

The one shortcoming in Table 2.5 is that it does not include any variables measuring the effect of economic conditions on vote choice. Given the prominence of economic conditions and economic evaluations in the two aggregate models discussed earlier, it seems appropriate to include similar variables in an individual-level model. Unfortunately, not until 1980 did the NES begin asking a consistent set of economic evaluation items. Even in these years, however, economic evaluations at the individual level are so strongly related to partisanship and presidential approval that they do not demonstrate consistently significant effects.[8]

One way to incorporate the national economic climate into the model is to pool respondents from all election years together and add a variable to the model that measures the state of the economy at the time of the election. In effect, a pooled model of this nature would be the same as that in Table 2.5, except that it would include a variable that describes the economic context of the election. This contextual influence should work in the following manner. In years when the economy is doing well all respondents should be more likely to vote for the incumbent presidential party, all else held equal, than in years when the economy is not doing well. In other words, even liberal Democrats are expected to be more likely to vote for an incumbent Republican president during a year when the economy is performing well than during a year when the economy is not performing well. These hypothetical liberal Democrats may still vote Democratic, but the probability of their voting Republican is affected by the national economic climate.

To test the economic context hypothesis, a variable measuring aggregate consumer expectations is added to the individual-level vote model. This variable is an index of consumer expectations that is based on a national survey taken every month by the Survey Research Center at the University of Michigan.[9] The index of consumer expectations measures how optimistic the public feels about the state of the economy. High values on the index indicate a positive outlook on the economy and low values indicate a pessimistic outlook on the economy. The level of economic optimism is expected to be positively related to the likelihood of voting for the incumbent presidential party.

Except for the addition of the consumer expectations variable, all variables in the pooled model are the same as in the analysis in Table 2.5. However, because the direction of the coefficients for many of the variables depends on the party of the presidency, it is necessary to control for the party in power. The Republicans held the White House in every presidential election between 1972 and 1992, with the exception of 1980. Therefore, it is expected that the coefficients for all variables with a partisan component—party identification, ideology, and the sociodemographic variables—will change signs in 1980, compared to the other years. To control for this in the pooled analysis, these variables are interacted with a party control variable, scored −1 for 1980 and +1 for all other years.

The results of the pooled analysis, presented in Table 2.6, confirm the economic context hypothesis: Even after controlling for myriad attitudinal and sociodemographic variables, the economic context of the election has a significant effect on voting behavior in presidential elections. Individual voters are more likely to vote for the incumbent party candidate in years when there is a high level of economic optimism than in years when the public is pessimistic about the economy, all else held equal. This finding is very much in keeping with the results of the aggregate analysis presented earlier in this chapter. The results for the other variables, along with the predictive capacity of the model—85.9% predicted correctly and a reduction in error of 71.7%—are very similar to what was found in Table 2.5

One difficulty with logistic regression lies in the interpretation of the coefficients. Logistic regression coefficients do not have the same standard linear interpretation as the coefficients from a linear regression model, where a unit change in one variable is associated with a certain number of units change in another variable. Instead, the most that can be said based on the logit coefficients in the first column in Table 2.6 is that changes in the independent variable increase or decrease the likelihood of a respondent voting for the incumbent party, depending on the sign of the coefficient of the variable. However, the antilogarithm of logit coefficient, presented as the odds ratio in the second column of Table 2.6, can be used to tell how much the odds of voting for the incumbent party change for a unit change in the independent variable (DeMaris 1993).

The interpretation of the odds ratio is straightforward. For instance, the ratio of the odds of a conservative voting Republican to the odds of a someone who is not conservative voting Republican is 2.296. This means that a conservative is approximately 2.3 times more likely to vote Republican than a voter who is not conservative, all else held constant. Odds ratios of less than one have the same interpretation. The ratio of the odds of a liberal voter voting Republican to the odds of a voter who is not liberal is .361 to 1; therefore, a liberal voter is only about a third as likely (because the ratio is less than one) to vote Republican than a voter who is not liberal.

Using the odds ratio as a basis for comparison, it is clear that some variables have much larger effects than others. With the exception of race,

Table 2.6   Pooled Analysis of Voting Behavior in Presidential Elections, 1972-1992 (Logistic Regression)

	b	*Odds Ratio*
Constant	−5.200***	—
Democrat	−1.446***	.236
Republican	1.093***	2.982
Liberal	−1.018***	.361
Conservative	.830***	2.296
Race	−1.729***	.178
Union	−.334***	.716
City	−.189*	.828
South	.264***	1.302
Approval	2.728***	15.295
Consumer expectations	.045***	1.046

Percentage correct = 85.9; PRE = .717; Model chi-square = 3,945.3; N = 5,384.
*$p < .10$ (two-tailed); ***$p < .01$ (two-tailed).

the other sociodemographic variables do not have a very strong relative effect on vote choice. The effect of race, however, is substantial: The odds of voting Republican are almost six times higher for voters who are not African American than for African American voters. Party identification and political ideology also have a significant effect on the odds of voting for the incumbent party; the effects are stronger for party identification, however, especially among Democrats. Clearly, however, the most influential determinant of voting behavior is presidential approval. Those who approve of the job the president is doing are more than fifteen times more likely to vote for the incumbent presidential party than those who do not approve of the way the president is handling the job. Compared to the other variables, this is an enormous effect.

How does the economic context of the election influence the odds of voting for the incumbent party? Unfortunately, direct comparisons between the odds ratio of the consumer expectations variable and the other variables are difficult to make. The problem with such comparisons is that the consumer expectations index is continuous and ranges from 68.9 in 1980 to 91.6 in 1984, whereas all of the other variables are dichotomous. A sense of how the economic context of the election influences voting behavior is still possible to obtain, however, by exploring how changes in the value of the consumer expectations index influence the odds of voting for the incumbent party. To figure how much the difference in economic expectations influenced the odds of voting for the incumbent party in 1984 versus 1980 (the two extremes), it is necessary to calculate the difference in the economic expectations index (22.7), multiply that number by the logit coefficient (22.7 • .045 = 1.022), and take the antilogarithm of that product ($e^{1.022}$). The resulting odds ratio is 2.78, which means that the odds of voting for the incumbent party were almost three times higher in 1984 than in 1980 for all voters, due to the difference in the level of confidence in the economy. This effect is not nearly as important as others, such as race and presidential approval, but it demonstrates that the economic context of an election significantly influences the likelihood of voters supporting the incumbent presidential party. The important fact to understand from this is that regardless of predisposition, as determined by political and demographic variables, all voters were more likely to support the incumbent in 1984 than in 1980 due to changes in aggregate economic perceptions.

The individual-level evidence presented in Tables 2.5 and 2.6 reinforces the idea that the vote decision is easily predicted based on a handful of variables. Although this is not a particularly new or innovative finding, the purpose of this analysis has been to demonstrate how one can argue that if campaign effects exist, they must be minimal, because most variation in voting behavior is accounted for by other variables.

Campaign Effects?

One of the difficulties with studying campaign effects at the individual level is that most surveys are not designed to study such effects. Part of the reason for this is that surveys are designed with a particular model of voting behavior in mind and the dominant models of voting behavior do not emphasize campaign effects. Nevertheless, the NES surveys do include some variables that can be used to examine campaign effects, albeit rather crudely. In particular, recall that the NES has asked respondents to identify how long before the election they made their vote decision; the choices range from those who knew all along to those who decided on election day. The NES has also asked respondents how many articles or stories they read, saw, or heard about the campaign in magazines and newspapers or on the radio and television.

Presumably, if the campaign has an effect on vote choice, the point during the campaign at which voters make their vote decision should have some effect on that decision. Those voters who knew all along how they would vote might be expected to have different preferences from those who made their decision at some point in the campaign, such as during the conventions or in the latter part of the campaign, due to the different degrees to which they were exposed to campaign information prior to making their vote decision. Also, those voters who are exposed to more campaign information via the mass media might be expected to express different candidate preferences from those with relatively little exposure; if the campaign messages have a net effect, that effect should be strongest among those with greater exposure to the campaign.

The data in Table 2.7 represent the zero-order correlation coefficients for the relationship between the dependent variable, vote decision, and the independent variables, time of vote decision and media exposure. The dependent variable is a dichotomous variable coded 1 for those voting for the incumbent party and 0 for those voting for other candidates. The variables for time of vote decision are also dichotomous variables, coded 1 for respondents who decided during the conventions or respondents who decided in the period between the conventions and election day and 0 for all other respondents. The media exposure variable is a simple count of the number of media sources from which the respondent reported getting information about the campaign. This variable ranges from 0 (no campaign information) to 4 (information from magazines, newspapers, radio, and television).[10]

The data in Table 2.7 provide only very limited support for possible campaign effects on vote choice. Only twelve of the twenty-two correlations between time of decision and vote choice are statistically significant and only four of the eleven correlations between media exposure and vote choice are statistically significant. There appears to be a slight tendency for those who decide how to vote late in the campaign to vote differently from the others. Even among those correlations that are statistically significant, however, none appear to represent a very substantial relationship.

These results are only suggestive, of course, because they represent only the bivariate relationships between campaign variables and vote choice. The effects found here are possibly spurious, due to the influence of unspecified variables. When the campaign variables are added to the model analyzed in Table 2.5 their effects (not shown here) change but still offer some support,

Table 2.7 Correlation Between Campaign Variables and Vote Choice in Presidential Elections, 1952-1992

	1952	1956	1960	1964	1968	1972	1976	1980	1984	1988	1992
Time of decision											
During conventions	-.09**	.01	.14**	.00	-.04	.07**	.07**	-.05	-.05	.00	-.08
Late in campaign	.07*	-.02	-.15***	-.18***	.03	-.17**	-.11**	-.08***	-.08**	-.01	-.17*
Media exposure	-.11**	.02	.10**	-.15***	-.02	.01	.04	-.12**	.01	.05	.04

*$p < .10$ (two-tailed); **$p < .05$ (two-tailed).

however meager, for significant campaign effects. In both 1976 and 1992, late deciders were significantly less likely to support the incumbent party than were those who made an earlier vote decision. In 1992, those who decided during the conventions were also significantly less likely to support the incumbent party. In 1988, media exposure was positively related to support for the incumbent party. All of these relationships are statistically significant (significance less than .05) even while controlling for the effect of other important variables. The best that can be said based on these results is that the campaign may, occasionally, have a slight effect on vote choice. Once again, this is not a resounding endorsement of strong campaign effects.

Conclusion

Most of the analysis presented in this chapter points in one direction: Election outcomes and voting behavior are easily explained with just a few variables, none of which are related to the campaign. Findings such as these are generally taken to indicate a limited, if any, role for campaigns to play in the electoral process. This is not, however, an inescapable conclusion. Analyses such as those presented in this chapter are designed to test specific ideas about the effect of personal characteristics, political attitudes, and national conditions—not the effect of campaigns—on voting behavior and election outcomes. Indeed, although such analyses certainly provide strong circumstantial evidence (by demonstrating the importance of other variables) that campaigns do not have an effect on elections, they provide no direct evidence because they are not designed to test for campaign effects. In the next chapter it is argued that most studies fail to uncover significant campaign effects because they are not looking for them. Only when there is a clear idea of what type of effect should be expected from campaigns and how one should look for that effect, can one successfully endeavor to search for campaign effects. This is the task that is taken up in the next chapter.

Notes

1. The presidential popularity figure was obtained from the Gallup Organization and the figure on public evaluations of the economy was taken from *Survey of Consumers: Historical Data,* The Survey Research Center, the University of Michigan.

2. The data sources used for change in GNP are Liesner (1989) for 1900 to 1928 and Darnay (1994) for 1932 to 1992.

3. The R^2 statistic is calculated as

$$\frac{(\text{Error without model}) - (\text{Error with model})}{(\text{Error without model})}$$

In other words, the reduction in error due to the regression model is expressed as a proportion of the original error. Hence, R^2 tells the proportional reduction in error associated with a particular regression model.

4. Data on presidential popularity were taken from Edwards and Gallup (1990) and from personal communications with the Gallup organization. Data on changes in personal finances were taken from *Surveys of Consumers: Historical Data,* Survey Research Center, the University of Michigan.

5. The coefficient for presidential popularity is only marginally significant. This is understandable given the small number of cases and the level of interitem correlation. The correlation between personal finances and popularity is .67 and the correlation between popularity and the tenure control variable is .51.

6. This idea is borrowed from Bartels (1992).

7. The exception to this is the 1980 National Election Study, which was designed with a three-wave panel component, making it more conducive to studying campaigns. Even with this innovation, however, the 1980 NES is of limited use for a detailed study of campaign effects (but see Finkel 1993).

8. In a separate analysis, both personal and national retrospective and prospective economic evaluations were added to the model for the years in which the questions were asked. The resulting coefficients were significant in only a few cases. These variables are excluded from Table 2.4 for the sake of parsimony and so that the same model can be tested for each year. However, for an analysis of the influence of personal finances on vote choice, see Markus (1988).

9. Consumer expectations data were taken from *Survey of Consumers: Historical Data,* Survey Research Center, the University of Michigan, Table 3. This measure of consumer expectations could not be used in the forecasting models in Tables 2.2 and 2.3 because observations for the spring months of presidential election years are not available until 1956.

10. In 1988, respondents were not asked how many stories about the campaign they had watched on television. Therefore, the media exposure variable ranges from 0 to 3 in 1988.

A Model of Campaign Effects

The evidence in Chapter 2 does not bode well for the thesis that presidential campaigns influence election outcomes. Based on just a few variables, none of which capture campaign effects, election outcomes and voting behavior are shown to be rather easily explained. These results fit very well with the findings of previous scholarship on presidential elections (see Lewis-Beck and Rice 1992). Yet these findings are also a bit unsettling. Can it really be that presidential election campaigns have so little to do with voting behavior and election outcomes?

Contemporary presidential campaigns generate enormous amounts of information intended to persuade voters and influence the election outcome. For the individual voter to escape the tentacles of campaign communications is very difficult. Evidence of the pervasive nature of campaign communication is that from 1952 to 1992 more than 97% of all voters report some exposure to the presidential campaign through either television, newspapers, magazines, or the radio.[1] Given the apparently ubiquitous nature of campaign information, how is it that campaigns appear to have so little influence on public opinion? The answer to this question is that campaigns *do* have an influence on public opinion. The problem is that, to this point, we have been looking in the wrong place for that influence. In the remainder of this book it is argued that despite all of the evidence presented in Chapter 2, campaigns play an important role in shaping public opinion about candidates during election years and ultimately play an important role in determining election outcomes.

The type of analysis presented in Chapter 2 is well suited to explaining aggregate outcomes or individual vote decisions on election day but it is not the type of analysis that is likely to capture campaign effects. Remember that election day is but one day in the entire presidential campaign process. Granted, it is the day that attracts the most attention and it is arguably the most consequential day of the process. However, by focusing on the ultimate outcome and ignoring the campaign period it is easy to misinterpret the process that led to that outcome. The necessary point to understand is that a political campaign is a process in which competing sides try to influence public opinion to the advantage of their candidate. Understanding the effect of any process is difficult if the focus is only on what comes out at the end of the process. Only by expanding the analysis to include studying the dynamics of public opinion during the campaign period can one gain an appreciation for the effect of the campaign.

A Model for Finding Campaign Effects

The search for campaign effects begins with what we already know: The ultimate outcome is predictable based on a few political and economic variables. What we do not know, however, is what role the campaign plays in moving public opinion to this point. A null (no effect) model of campaign effects implies constancy of public opinion during the campaign. If the campaign process is irrelevant, we would expect to see relative constancy in public opinion during the campaign period. In other words, the level of support for candidates should be roughly the same throughout the course of the campaign as it is at the endpoint, election day; what happens during the campaign should matter very little to the level of candidate support.

Figure 3.1 illustrates the null model of campaign effects. This figure presents the pattern of candidate support (measured with trial-heat polls) over the course of a hypothetical 120-day campaign period. The important thing to note here is that the level of candidate support is fairly constant across the campaign period with the exception of only minor, seemingly random perturbations. The hypothetical campaign events depicted in Figure

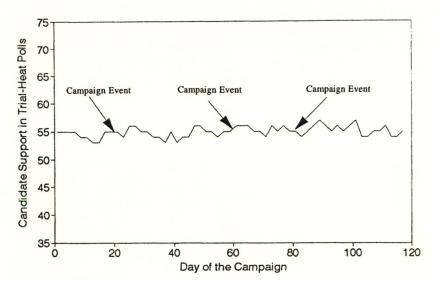

Figure 3.1. The Null Model of Campaign Effects in a Hypothetical Campaign

3.1 do not appear to alter the pattern of candidate support, which indicates that there are no campaign effects. To some extent the pattern displayed in Figure 3.1 is implied by the evidence of predictable outcomes presented in Chapter 2. If variables measured in the spring of the election before the general election campaign really begins accurately predict the outcome, then opinion must be fairly constant during the campaign period.

The null model does not, however, square well with what we know about public opinion during the campaign. In fact, there is significant movement in public opinion during the campaign season. A number of scholars have documented the changes in both candidate preference (Gelman and King 1993; Kiewiet and Rivers 1985) and partisanship (Allsop and Weisberg 1988; Weisberg and Allsop 1990) during the campaign. However, demonstrating that public opinion fluctuates during the campaign is not a sufficient condition for demonstrating campaign effects. Indeed, changes in opinion during a campaign season could be in response to any number of factors, including noncampaign stimuli. For instance, Kiewiet and Rivers (1985) found that changes in support for Reagan (as measured with trial-heat polls) during the 1984 campaign were closely tied to changes in the unemployment rate, which is clearly not a campaign influence.

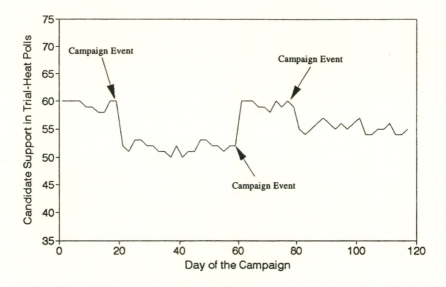

Figure 3.2. Significant Event Effects in a Hypothetical Campaign

For changes in public opinion to be indicative of campaign effects, it is necessary to demonstrate first that there is significant fluctuation in public opinion and second that the changes observed are in response to the occurrence of campaign events. Ideally, this means that shifts in opinion must be relatively proximate to the preceding occurrence of a campaign-related event. A pattern of this type is displayed in Figure 3.2, which shows the pattern of candidate support during the same hypothetical 120-day campaign period as depicted in Figure 3.1. The pattern in Figure 3.2 reveals some of the same random changes in opinion that are found in Figure 3.1. The difference, however, is that there are three relatively pronounced shifts in candidate support that coincide with the occurrence of hypothetical campaign events. Shifts in opinion such as these are strongly suggestive of significant campaign effects.

Even if the type of effects shown in Figure 3.2 do exist, however, it is necessary to recognize that there may be limits to the potential magnitude of these effects on the final outcome. Based on the analysis in Chapter 2, it is reasonable to assume that there is something resembling an equilibrium level of support for presidential candidates. The term *equilibrium* is used because there are thought to be forces exogenous to the campaign that push (or pull) the level of candidate support to a certain "natural" outcome.[2] In other words, in each election year there exists an outcome toward which the public is naturally predisposed. This natural predisposition is thought to be a function of prevailing national conditions. In effect, the equilibrium outcome is analogous to Converse's (1966) "normal" vote concept except that in this case the normal vote (outcome) is determined by national conditions rather than by party identification.

The equilibrium level of candidate support can be viewed as something like the expected outcome, based on forecasting models such as the one presented in Chapter 2. This equilibrium is easily predicted and is expected to change from one election year to the next depending on prevailing national conditions. In a year such as 1980, with a sluggish economy and an unpopular president, the equilibrium is expected to favor the challenging party. In a year such as 1984, with a growing economy and a popular president, the equilibrium is expected to favor the incumbent party. Around this equilibrium level we expect to see campaign-induced shifts in public opinion. In the end, it is expected that the forces of the campaign do influence public opinion but in such a way that the ultimate outcome is close to the expected equilibrium outcome. In effect, it is argued here that campaigns and national conditions jointly produce election outcomes.

An illustration of the joint effects of campaign events and national conditions is presented in Figure 3.3. The left panel of Figure 3.3 presents the effect of campaign events on support for a candidate in a hypothetical campaign during a year when national conditions are favorable for that candidate's party. This panel is actually just a replication of the pattern displayed in Figure 3.2. The horizontal line in the panel indicates the equilibrium, or expected outcome, based on prevailing national conditions. Note that there is a significant amount of movement in public opinion during the campaign but, in the end, the outcome is as expected (the equilibrium outcome). The panel on the right depicts the effects of campaign events on the same candidate but in a year when national conditions are unfavorable for the candidate's party. The horizontal line in this panel also indicates the equilibrium, or expected outcome, which is 10 percentage points lower than it was under favorable national conditions. What is particularly important to glean from this panel is that even though the equilibrium level of candidate support is different in the two panels, the pattern of candidate support on the right is exactly the same as the pattern on the left. In both cases, campaign events have a significant effect on fluctuations in public opinion, but the

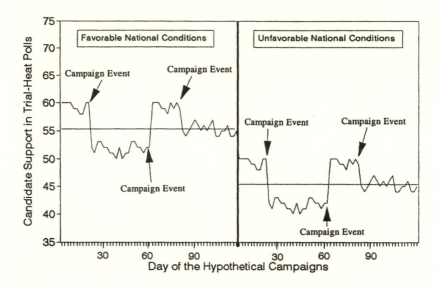

Figure 3.3. Identical Event Effects Under Different National Conditions

shifts in opinion that are caused by events tend to hover around the equilibrium level of candidate support.

Note that Figure 3.3 is set up to emphasize the importance of the concept of an equilibrium outcome; therefore, the eventual outcome is very close to the equilibrium outcome. This will not always be the case. The cumulative effect of campaign events will, at times, possibly produce outcomes that deviate significantly from the equilibrium outcome. The important point is that it is expected that there is a natural tendency for opinion to move toward the equilibrium outcome during the campaign; and it is this tendency that campaigns either work with or fight against. The equilibrium outcome, then, may reflect the degree to which candidates have to wage a strong campaign to win or improve their standing. However, the strength of the campaign effort may also play a role in determining how close the actual outcome is to the equilibrium outcome.

One conclusion that can be reached from Figure 3.3 is that it is not contradictory to have both strong campaign effects on public opinion *and* highly predictable election outcomes. In fact it is expected that campaigns and equilibrium both play an important role in shaping election outcomes.

Hypotheses

This view of the role of campaigns and national conditions suggests the following general hypotheses.

H1: There exists an equilibrium level of candidate support during presidential campaigns and this level of support is a function of exogenous (noncampaign) national political and economic variables.

H2: During the campaign season public opinion will deviate, sometimes widely, from the equilibrium level of candidate support. Variations in candidate support during the campaign season are largely attributable to the occurrence of campaign events.

H3: There are rarely significant changes in national political and economic conditions during the campaign; therefore, national conditions have very little effect on changes in public opinion during the campaign.

Given the accuracy of the forecasting model presented in Chapter 2, the first hypothesis is quite clear. A large part of public support for the candidates is clearly determined by noncampaign factors. Based on prevailing national conditions, it is expected that there is a natural tendency toward a certain level of candidate support. This level is referred to here as the equilibrium level of support because it can be viewed as the level that is "natural," given prevailing national conditions. This hypothesis does not require a completely deterministic electorate, devoid of all free will—only an expected level of candidate support based on the prior behavior of the electorate.

The second and third hypotheses make it clear that although there may be an equilibrium level of candidate support, public opinion is not expected to be constant during the campaign season. Instead, it is expected that public opinion during the campaign season is fluid and highly responsive to the occurrence of campaign events. Specifically, when events occur that are expected to favor one candidate over the other, such as a party nominating convention or a strong debate performance, there should be a subsequent positive change in support for that candidate. In short, it is expected that the pattern of public opinion during the campaign season is more similar to that displayed in Figures 3.2 and 3.3 than in Figure 3.1.

According to the third hypothesis, changes in national conditions during the campaign season are not expected to have a strong influence on changes in public opinion. The primary reason for this hypothesis is that national conditions, such as the state of the economy or presidential popularity, do not exhibit very much variation over the course of a few months. What this implies is that the national context of the election is fairly constant throughout the campaign period. National conditions are expected to exhibit the greatest variation and the greatest influence across election years, not during an election year.

The Role of Information

Even if the subsequent analysis supports the preceding hypotheses, one might reasonably ask how these effects are manufactured. What is the process that produces the type of effects previously described? To understand the process by which these effects are produced, it helps to recall the primary function of presidential campaigns: to generate information for the purpose of persuasion. The target of these efforts of persuasion is the voting public. To illustrate how voters might be persuaded by campaign information, the next section describes an information processing model that seems particularly appropriate for the campaign process. This is followed by a discussion of why the voting public is not only susceptible to persuasion but also in great need of the information generated by campaigns.

HOW CAMPAIGN INFORMATION IS PROCESSED

The information processing model that best fits the description of how campaign events influence public opinion is the "on-line" (OL) or "impression-driven" model of candidate evaluation (Lodge, McGraw, and Stroh 1989; Lodge, Steenbergen, and Brau 1995; Lodge and Stroh 1993). According to the on-line model, voters begin the campaign with a general impression of the candidates based on what they know about the candidates at that point. As events unfold and the voter is presented with more information about the candidates, this information is incorporated into the voter's *events tally*. The events tally, also referred to as an evaluation tally, is "conceived as a counter in working memory that integrates new information into a 'running tally' of one's current impression" (Lodge, McGraw, and Stroh 1989, 401). In other words, the information generated over time by the campaign is used to update the voter's impression of the candidates as it is received. According to Lodge et al., "From the OL perspective, 'responsive voters' will decrease their general evaluation of a candidate when confronted with negative information and increase their candidate evaluations when made aware of information that they judge to be positive" (Lodge, Steenbergen, and Brau 1995, 311).

The on-line information processing model fits well with the nature of campaign events discussed earlier in this chapter: As events unfold, it is expected that the information they generate will have an effect on voters' candidate evaluations and cause a corresponding shift in candidate support toward the candidate favored by the event. When the next important event occurs, it is expected that mass opinion will again shift in the direction of the candidate favored by that event. For example, suppose that on one day revelations of a scandal in the Democratic campaign are made in the media. Following such an "event," it is reasonable to expect a shift in mass opinion in favor of the Republican candidate as voters incorporate this information into their running tally. Now suppose that several days later it is revealed that there was no substance to the charges and the Democratic candidate launches a fierce attack on his opponent, accusing him or her of "mudslinging." This new information might be expected to be incorporated into voters' running tally so that public opinion would shift back toward the Democratic candidate. The process is expected to work in much the same way as depicted in these two examples: Voters stay "on-line" during the campaign and update their evaluations of the candidates as events unfold and new information is made available to them. If voters process information in this fashion, then it is reasonable to expect to see corresponding shifts in candidate support following the occurrence of significant campaign events.

Given that there are a number of alternative models of voter information acquisition and decision making, one could reasonably question whether the on-line model is necessarily the most appropriate model for this analysis. Because most other models of voter decision making are "memory-based, moment-of-decision" models (Lau 1995, 181), however, they are not as appropriate for the analysis of campaigns as the on-line model. Memory-based, moment-of-decision models assume that voters make a decision, presumably at the end of the campaign, based on retrieval of relevant information from long-term memory.[3] The on-line model, on the other hand, assumes only that voters process information as it is received and adjust their evaluations in accordance with the new information. If voters actually do store information in long-term memory to be retrieved at the end of the campaign, there would be no clear connection between the occurrence of campaign events and corresponding shifts in candidate support. Voters would simply wait until the end of the campaign and make their decision on the basis of information culled from the entire campaign. The on-line model, however, is very consistent with the idea of campaign events leading to shifts in candidate support. In fact, the on-line model assumes that voters are constantly updating their evaluations as new information is received. Of course, these evaluations are assumed to translate into votes.

THE FUNCTION OF INFORMATION

Suggesting that on-line information processing leads to strong campaign effects hinges on one crucial assumption: The information acquired during the campaign serves a valuable function for the voters. If the information acquired is information the voters already have or is irrelevant to most voters, then it is unlikely to affect the typical voter's running tally. Support for the assumption that campaign information is valuable to voters is found in the work of other scholars, especially the work of Popkin (1991) and Gelman and King (1993), who have studied the role of information in political campaigns. Recall from the discussion in Chapter 1 that Popkin (1991) describes voters as having limited information about candidates and issues in the campaign. Most voters pay very little attention to politics and public affairs between elections and hence are in need of information with which they can make an "informed" decision. There is a high level of demand for information about candidates and issues, information that is readily provided by the campaigns. This provides the campaigns with an opportunity to influence voters via campaign communications. Despite increasing negativity concerning the role of campaigns in American politics, Popkin asserts that campaigns serve a very fundamental democratic function: providing voters with much-needed information.

The work of Gelman and King (1993) is most directly related to this analysis. Gelman and King make the observation that even though election outcomes are easily predicted, there is a lot of movement in public opinion polls during the campaign season and these changes in mass opinion can be tied to patterns of campaign communication.[4] As campaign events occur, the public is provided with more information about the candidates and issues. This information is then incorporated into the decision-making process and members of the mass public are in a better position to make informed decisions, which results in changes in public opinion.

The most important contribution of Gelman and King's work is the connection they make between the information-generating function of campaigns and the predictability of voting behavior and election outcomes. According to Gelman and King, as the campaign progresses more and more information about candidates and issues is provided through the media. As voters absorb this information they become more enlightened about the choices available to them. As voters become more enlightened their behavior becomes more predictable, because *enlightenment* means that voters become more sensitive to the types of variables that usually dominate voting behavior: partisanship, presidential performance, and the state of the economy (Gelman and King 1993, 433-35). In the end, according to Gelman and King, the campaign provides the information necessary for voters to make informed choices and informed choices lead to predictable outcomes. Campaign communications, then, by providing much-needed information, help bring public opinion into equilibrium. Of course, as Gelman and King point out, this hypothesis is dependent on both parties running relatively effective campaigns (1993, 449). If one side runs a vastly superior campaign, then the campaign could generate an outcome significantly different from the outcome expected.

This view of campaigns is very similar to the view espoused by Markus (1988) in his article on the relationship between economic conditions and voting behavior. According to Markus, although the referendum voting models make the campaign appear to be inefficacious, the campaign may be "a very important vehicle for heightening voter awareness of prevailing economic conditions and the electoral relevance thereof" (1988, 152). In other words, it may be campaigns and the information they generate that make elections so predictable. Conclusions such as these are likely to be overlooked, however, by analyses that focus only on the end game—election day.

Central to all investigations of the information-generating aspect of the campaign is the role of the mass media (Gelman and King 1993; Popkin 1991). A campaign event that occurs in isolation and is not reported to the public is similar to the tree that falls in the woods: It makes a sound only if someone is there to hear it. According to Gelman and King, the media play an important role in making election outcomes as predictable as they are by reporting on the activities—speeches, conventions, debates, accusations, issue positions—of the campaign and, in the process, helping the voter make "enlightened" choices (1993, 448-49).

This discussion of the role of campaign information fits well with the notion of a preexisting equilibrium level of candidate support offered in the first hypothesis. If we accept that there exists an equilibrium level of candidate support (to borrow a term from Gelman and King, we might even refer to this as the "enlightened" level of support) and that the function of campaign information is to bring opinion into equilibrium, then it is plausible to suggest that the potential magnitude of campaign effects is constrained by the electoral equilibrium. Suppose, for example, that the Republican party share of the equilibrium vote in a given election is 55%. Now suppose that, early in the campaign, the Republican candidate is averaging 51% in the trial-heat polls. Given that there is not a great deficit between the equilibrium vote and the preelection trial-heat polls, there is not a lot of room for improvement; in other words, campaign events probably will not have a strong effect on public opinion in a case such as this. On the other hand, if pre-election polls showed the Republicans with a substantially larger support deficit (or surplus), we might expect stronger campaign effects because public opinion is further out of equilibrium. This idea is similar to that offered by Aldrich (1993), who suggests that national conditions may not only determine the context of the campaign but may limit the number of feasible campaign strategies and the potential effectiveness of these strategies.

Based on this view of the role of equilibrium, the following additional hypothesis is offered:

H4:   The magnitude of the effect of campaign events on public opinion during the campaign is partially dependent on the disparity between the level of support for the candidate at the time of the event and the expected election outcome. Specifically, the greater the negative disparity (running behind the expected level of support), the greater the potential effect of a positive campaign event.

Note that this effect is expected to be asymmetric. If presidential candidates are running a significant opinion deficit—poll standings well below the expected level—there is greater capacity for orchestrated campaign activity to increase their poll standing than if they were running a significant opinion surplus—poll standings well above the expected level. When a candidate is running an opinion deficit, there is a larger supply of untapped, potentially sympathetic supporters available to receive the campaign messages and incorporate them into their evaluations than when a candidate runs an opinion surplus. Of course, one candidate's surplus is another candidate's

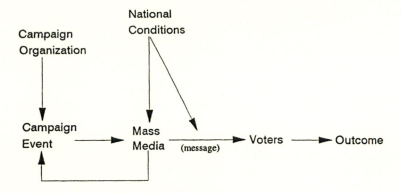

Figure 3.4. Diagram of the Campaign Process

deficit, so it can generally be said that the further out of equilibrium public opinion is, the greater the potential for strong campaign effects.

Needless to say, many other factors can influence the effect of a given campaign event. For instance, different types of events can be expected to generate different types of responses. A nominating convention, for example, is likely to produce more positive publicity and hence a greater shift in opinion than will a major policy speech. Also, some events will be better coordinated than others and should receive a more positive public response. The important point is that two events of roughly the same "quality" can produce different responses depending on how much potential there is for gain or loss in the polls. This potential can be roughly understood as the disparity between a candidate's standing in the polls and that candidate's equilibrium vote share.

The Campaign Process

Based on the preceding four hypotheses and the discussion of the role of information in political campaigns, the diagram in Figure 3.4 depicts the campaign process. This diagram is not intended to capture all aspects of the campaign process but is intended to be a simple portrayal of the interaction between the main actors and influences in the process. Several important connections are depicted in the diagram. Campaign organizations, in the process of running the campaign, produce campaign events intended to influence the voters. These events range in magnitude from conventions and debates to vice presidential selection and stump speeches, and are mediated through the mass media. Very few voters experience campaign events firsthand. Instead, for most voters the information or message about the event is transmitted through some media outlet. As Popkin (1991) and Gelman and King (1993) point out, the media provide the link between the campaign and the electorate.

To some extent, the media are also able to produce campaign events, or at least magnify aspects of the campaign to which the candidates must react. An example of this might be a story about some aspect of the candidate's personal life or public record, perhaps of a scandalous nature. Stories about allegations of marital infidelity and draft evasion on the part of Bill Clinton in 1992 certainly fit into this category. Other examples of this type of media event are the questions raised about Dan Quayle's National Guard service in 1988 or Geraldine Ferraro's tax problems in 1984. In each of these cases, significant issues about the candidates' backgrounds were raised and became part of the campaign. The media, of course, do not manufacture these events, but by magnifying certain issues they do produce campaign events to which the campaigns must react.

National conditions, such as the state of the economy or the performance of the incumbent administration, are also important to the process. The most obvious way that national conditions influence the process is by influencing the vote. Again, though, this influence is likely to be mediated through press and television coverage. Although some voters may make judgments about national conditions and hence the candidates based on their own personal experience, most voters receive information about the economy, foreign policy, and presidential performance through the mass media. Frequently, the information generated by the media about national conditions comes from the political campaigns as they try to heighten voters' awareness of the issues and personalities in the campaign. Another important role for national conditions (illustrated by the arrow running from national conditions to the media message) is their influence on the magnitude of the effect campaign events are likely to produce, as suggested in the fourth hypothesis.

Finally, at the end of the process voters use the information they have acquired and incorporate it into their running tally of candidate evaluations, which they can then use to help them decide for whom to vote. Voters, of course, are also motivated by other factors, such as partisanship, ideology, race, religion, and issue positions, but the information they receive during the campaign may affect the weight they give to these factors.

Information Trends in Presidential Campaigns

The preceding discussion of the effect of campaigns hinges on the role of information. Specifically, campaign events are thought to produce changes in public opinion by providing the public with information that is relevant to the vote decision. This discussion implies that there is a pattern to the flow of information during the campaign, with more information generated as events unfold. Specifically, one might expect more information to be generated by major events, such as the conventions and debates, and during the fall when the campaigns are running at full throttle.

Figure 3.5 displays the pattern of campaign communications during the 1984, 1988, and 1992 campaigns, respectively. What these figures present is the average daily number of paragraphs about the campaign on the front page of the *New York Times* for seven-day periods from June 1 through election day.[5] Although the *New York Times* is only one of the countless number of media sources through which people might get information, it is one of the leading newspapers in the country and it is likely to reflect the general pattern of campaign communication found in other media sources. Although specific content may differ from day to day, the assumption made here is that, over time, the trend in the amount of coverage in the *New York Times* is similar to that found in most media sources.

Although there are some differences, a similar pattern of communication emerges in all three years. Relatively little campaign information is generated in the early part of the summer, but there are substantial spikes in the amount of information generated during the time of the party nominating conventions. This holds true for both the Democratic and Republican conventions. During the period between the conventions, the level of information subsides. There is also a brief period of declining information following the second convention but a gradual increase in information during the fall campaign. Although there may be information spikes associated with the occurrence of the debates later in the campaign, this is hard to distinguish because the level of information tends to be fairly high throughout the fall campaign.

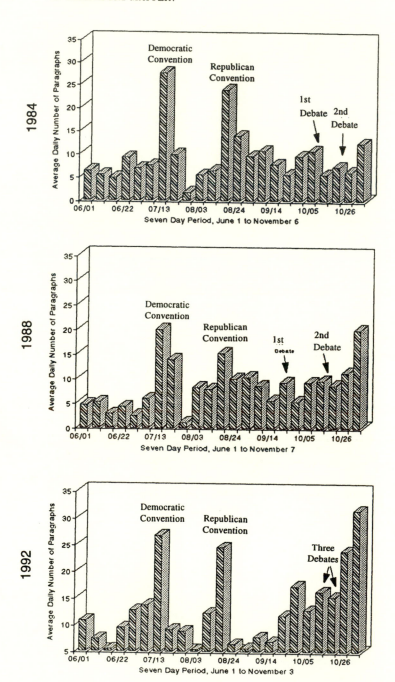

Figure 3.5. Front-Page *New York Times* Presidential Campaign Coverage, 1984-1992

Table 3.1   The Relationship Between Campaign Events and Front-Page *New York Times* Coverage of the Campaign, 1984-1992 (GLS Results)

	1984 b	1988 b	1992 b
Constant	7.364*	5.998*	7.058*
	(.723)	(.816)	(1.034)
Democratic convention	16.437*	9.575*	15.306*
	(2.51)	(2.592)	(2.826)
Republican convention	14.945*	8.647*	14.736*
	(2.382)	(2.592)	(2.826)
First presidential debate	7.158*	0.778	−1.565
	(3.468)	(3.564)	(4.808)
Second presidential debate	0.883	−0.212	−0.349
	(3.55)	(3.626)	(5.494)
Third presidential debate	—	—	−1.190
	—	—	(4.213)
Vice presidential debate	0.751	0.976	−3.397
	(3.491)	(3.591)	(5.201)
Fall campaign	−0.011	.104*	.243*
	(.030)	(.031)	(.040)
N	158	159	154
R^2	0.36	0.16	0.34
Durbin-Watson	1.99	1.95	1.859

NOTE: GLS estimates were derived using the Yule-Walker method for correction of serial correlation. Standard errors are in parentheses.
*$p < .05$ (two-tailed).

There are some differences in the patterns of campaign communication in the three years. For instance, the uptick in coverage in the fall is most apparent in 1992 and least apparent in 1984. There are also differences in the overall amount of coverage given to each of the campaigns; the average daily number of paragraphs was 9.1 in 1984, 8.5 in 1988, and 12.6 in 1992. No doubt, part of the explanation for the high level of coverage in 1992 is that for at least part of the campaign there were three major candidates.

A more systematic analysis of the patterns of campaign communication from 1984 to 1992 is found in Table 3.1, which presents a regression analysis of the determinants of the level of campaign coverage. This analysis is based on daily counts of campaign paragraphs rather than the weekly averages presented in Figure 3.5. The dependent variable in this analysis is the number of campaign paragraphs on the front page of the *New York Times* on each day of the analysis. The independent variables are dummy variables for the party conventions (coded 1 for the period between two days before and three days after the conventions and 0 for all other days), dummy variables for the presidential debates (coded 1 for the day of the debate and the two days following the debate and 0 for all other days), and a counter variable for the increasing activity in the fall campaign (coded 0 for all days prior to September 1 and taking on an increasing value, in increments of 1, for each successive day).

The results in Table 3.1 support the conclusion that there is a fairly similar pattern of communication in each of the three election years. The conventions provide a significant and large bump in the amount of information generated. In addition, in each of the three years the first convention, which was also the Democratic and challenging-party convention, generates slightly more information than does the second convention. The debates, on the other hand, do not appear to generate significantly more information than was being generated on other days around the time of the debates. The one exception to this is the first debate of 1984, which had a significant positive effect on the amount of campaign information. Assessing the independent effects of debates on information flow is difficult, however, because the debates occur during the busiest time of the campaign, when there is generally a lot of information being generated on a daily basis. Interestingly, there was a clear pattern of increasing amounts of information as the fall campaign progressed in 1988 and 1992 but not in 1984. Note that in 1984, when the fall campaign did not display an increase in information levels, there was a significant debate effect on the level of information.

Finally, although the model of campaign coverage produced several significant findings, the R^2 statistics indicate that much of the variation in campaign coverage remains to be explained.[6] The intention of this brief analysis is not, however, to provide an exhaustive explanation of campaign coverage. Instead, this analysis is intended only to illustrate that the amount of campaign information given to the public varies systematically with the major activities of the campaign.

The pattern displayed in Figure 3.5 makes it quite clear that there are periods of the campaign in which relatively little information is communicated

—primarily, with the exception of the weeks of the convention, during the summer—and periods when substantial amounts of information are communicated—primarily during the conventions and during the fall campaign period. Another useful way to think about the flow of information is in terms of the cumulative amount of campaign information at any given point in time. As the campaign progresses, the cumulative amount of information being transmitted increases from day to day. Given this, as time goes on, information is less and less scarce for the information consumers—voters. Therefore, it might be expected that there are diminishing returns to the value of information over the course of the campaign. As the campaign progresses, the supply of information increases, voters incorporate more and more into their evaluation tallies, and the demand for information should decrease as the needs of the voters are satisfied. As a result, the value of each additional piece of information should be smaller than that of preceding pieces of information. The demand for information might also decline as the campaign progresses because many voters will use the information they have consumed and make an early vote decision. Having made this decision, additional information will be of little value to these voters.

The following hypothesis is based on these ideas about the declining value of information over the course of the campaign.

H5: Because the value of information declines as the cumulative amount of information increases, events that occur early in the campaign period have greater potential to influence voters than do events of equivalent quality that occur later in the campaign.

Note that this hypothesis does not suggest that all events occurring early in the campaign will have a greater effect on public opinion than all events that occur later in the campaign, only that events that are qualitatively equal are expected to have a greater effect if they occur early in the campaign rather than late.

Expectations

Based on the discussion and analysis presented in this chapter, the expectations for the remaining chapters are clear. Campaign events are expected to have an effect on public opinion: This effect is to influence changes in candidate preference during the campaign period. Two matters concerning this have been left unclear to this point: the manner in which campaign events and the campaign period are defined. There are probably about as many definitions of what constitutes an *event* as there are events. After all, events are always occurring; with each passing moment of a political campaign it can be said that another event has occurred. Although a more complete description of how events are defined and selected is presented in Chapter 6, several different types of events will clearly be included in the analysis. First, there are highly visible events, such as nominating conventions and presidential debates. If these "marquee" events have no effect on public opinion there seems to be little reason to look elsewhere. Second, there are less visible but presumably still consequential events that are produced by the campaigns, such as vice presidential candidate announcements, major campaign speeches, high-visibility endorsements, and calculated campaign stunts that receive a lot of exposure. There are also events that "happen" to campaigns, such as major campaign gaffes and scandals. Another category of events includes those that occur outside the campaign, such as scandals involving a member of the administration, or a foreign policy action. These, of course, are not campaign events per se but are still events that might be expected to influence candidate preference. The effects of all of these different types of events are analyzed in the following chapters.

There are also a number of different ways in which one can define the campaign period. Denton and Stuckey, for instance, in their discussion of the 1992 campaign, make a distinction between the preprimary phase, the primary phase, the convention phase, and the general election phase of the campaign (Denton and Stuckey 1994, 10-18). These distinctions, although serving Denton and Stuckey's purposes well, are not appropriate for the analysis conducted here. In this analysis, the campaign period of interest is the general election period, which is defined as the period between the last primary and election day. The general election campaign is defined in this way for a number of reasons. First, the identity of the two major party candidates is usually known by this point and attention shifts to the differences between these candidates. Second, the nominating conventions and the events leading up to them receive more attention (see Figure 3.5 and Table 3.1) and, therefore, could be capable of producing more significant shifts in public opinion than any other events in the campaign. To define the general election period as beginning after the conventions would preclude an analysis of what may be the most important events of the campaign.

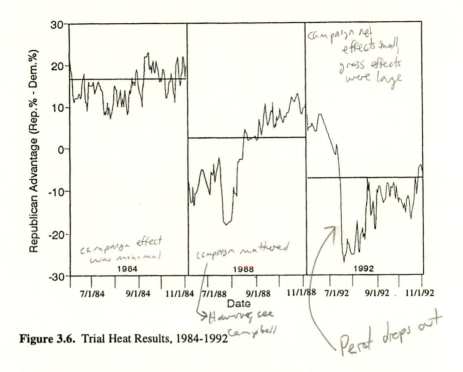

Figure 3.6. Trial Heat Results, 1984-1992

In addition to the effects of campaign events, it is expected that national conditions play a very important but different role in shaping the eventual outcome. First, national conditions are expected to determine the equilibrium, or expected, level of candidate support during the campaign. Second, there is some interaction between national conditions and the effect of campaign events: The potential effect of campaign events is expected to be constrained by the equilibrium election outcomes, as determined by prevailing national conditions. Because campaign events are hypothesized to function in such a way as to bring opinion into equilibrium, they should demonstrate the greatest effect when opinion is significantly out of equilibrium.

The ideas presented in this chapter are subjected to empirical scrutiny in the remainder of this book. Before proceeding to the more detailed analyses, however, Figure 3.6 provides an initial glimpse of the degree to which the hypotheses in this chapter might be borne out by data from the past three presidential campaigns. The data in Figure 3.6 represent the ebb and flow of candidate support over the course of the 1984, 1988, and 1992 presidential campaigns. Specifically, the vertical axis represents the Republican candidate's percentage point advantage over the Democratic candidate in preelection trial-heat (candidate preference) polls (see Appendix A for a complete explanation of how these data were gathered). Positive values on the vertical axis indicate a Republican lead in the polls and negative values indicate a Democratic lead. The date of the trial-heat polls is displayed across the horizontal axis for a period from early June to just before the election in November for each of the three elections. The meandering line throughout Figure 3.6 represents the daily readings from the trial heat polls, and the flat horizontal lines (one for each year) represent the equilibrium, or expected election outcomes. These expected outcomes are based on prevailing national conditions and derived from estimates provided by the spring forecasting model in Chapter 2.

Several aspects of Figure 3.6 lend initial support to the hypotheses specified in this chapter. First, public opinion is anything but constant throughout the three campaign periods. In each of the three years there is significant variation in candidate support over the course of the campaign. More important, at certain points in each campaign there are abrupt and substantial shifts in candidate support. This is consistent with significant campaign effects, as described earlier in this chapter. The pattern of candidate support in each of the three years is much more similar to the pattern displayed in Figure 3.2, which presented significant event effects, than in Figure 3.1, which presented the null model. However, as indicated earlier, documenting such a pattern is not a sufficient condition for demonstrating campaign effects; it remains to be seen whether these shifts in candidate support coincide with the occurrence of important campaign events. Second, there is a tendency to find much more dramatic swings in public opinion in the early part of the campaign than in the later part, especially in 1988 and 1992. A pattern of this nature may indicate stronger campaign effects in the early part of the campaign, as suggested in the fifth hypothesis. Again, though, it remains to be seen whether this pattern is associated with campaign activity.

Third, although there is significant variation in public opinion during each of the campaign years, that variation appears to hover around and gravitate toward the equilibrium level of candidate support. This tendency in the data is very similar to that displayed in Figure 3.3, which illustrated the joint effect of campaign events and national conditions on public opinion. This pattern provides strong support for the idea that there is an equilibrium level of support in an election year toward which campaigns help to move public opinion, and that equilibrium constrains the effect of campaign events. Note that by the end of the campaign candidate support is close to the point predicted by the equilibrium outcome, which may indicate strong national effects. Also note, however, that there is some discrepancy between the equilibrium outcome and the level of candidate support at the end of the campaign in each of the years—the discrepancy is particularly pronounced in 1988 and less so in 1992. This may indicate the net effects of the campaigns above and beyond the effect of national conditions.

Based on the pattern of candidate support found in Figure 3.6, there appears to be some cause for optimism as the search for campaign effects begins in earnest. There is also reason for caution, however, as the quick perusal of the data provided here is meant only to suggest its potential for demonstrating campaign effects. Before any firm conclusions can be reached, the data presented in Figure 3.6, along with data from several other sources, require much closer scrutiny. In the following chapters, a more thorough analysis of the role of campaigns in presidential elections is conducted. As will become apparent, in some cases the data are plentiful and the conclusions are clear. In other cases, the data are not quite as plentiful and the conclusions require greater caution. In all cases, however, there is something to be learned about the role of campaigns in presidential elections.

Notes

1. This figure is derived from the American National Election Studies Cumulative Data File, 1952-1992 (ICPSR study #8475). The figure reported here does not include respondents from 1988 because those respondents were not asked if they had any exposure to the campaign via television. Respondents in 1988 are assumed to not systematically differ from respondents in other years, in terms of media exposure.

2. The term *equilibrium* may take on a different meaning in different contexts. For instance, for people who study formal theory it has a very clear technical meaning that is different from the way it is used here. Using it differently in this analysis is not intended to deny other meanings of equilibrium, or to suggest that this is the only correct use of the word.

3. Most research shows that voters do not retain much specific information in their long-term memory.

4. One conclusion Gelman and King (1993) draw from their work is that because they demonstrate so much fluctuation and because they represent "unenlightened" opinions, early trial-heat polls are meaningless indicators of presidential preference. Their point is well taken only if the question is to what degree early polls can predict the actual election outcome. However, for

an analysis that focuses on how public opinion changes during the campaign, early polls are very useful; they represent candidate preferences at a point in time given the level of campaign activity and the amount of information available to the voters at that time. The key question is, how does campaign activity and hence the flow of information affect candidate standings in the polls and, ultimately, the election outcome?

5. The count is the number of campaign paragraphs, partial or full, that appeared on the front page. Photographs and figures, such as poll results, were counted as paragraphs. To be included in the count a story had to be about a candidate or personality involved in the campaign (including family members), issue positions, issues within the party, or public opinion toward any aspect of the campaign. Because incumbent presidents receive coverage for activities not related to the campaign, only those stories that are clearly about the campaign are counted.

6. When a lagged dependent variable is added to the model, the explained variance increases but the relationships found in Table 3.1 do not appreciably change.

Nominating Conventions

The national political parties have been meeting in nominating conventions during presidential election years since the early 1830s. The conventions of today, however, are very different from those of the 1800s. Ostensibly, party conventions today still gather to do the important party business of drafting a platform and nominating the presidential and vice presidential candidates. However, most of the suspense of the nomination and most of the squabbling over what will be in the party platform is over before the convention begins (Wayne 1992, 137). As a result, today's conventions are criticized as being "nonevents" precisely because so many of the important decisions have been made ahead of time. This is a significant break from conventions of the past, a break that seems to have occurred following the conventions of 1952. Prior to this point, party conventions were more appropriately described as deliberative meetings in which party leaders gathered to debate and negotiate among themselves and eventually choose a national ticket (Wayne 1992, 137). Frequently, this was not an easy process, sometimes requiring several ballots before a candidate could be chosen. Indeed, from 1831 to 1952 there were 26 (10 Republican and 16 Democratic) conventions at which it was necessary to go to more than one ballot to select the presidential nominee. There have been no second (or later) ballot nominations since the 1952 Democratic convention (*Congressional Quarterly* 1987).

Although many of the important decisions may be made before the party convenes, the contemporary convention still serves very important electoral functions for the party. The primary function of the contemporary convention is to generate an image of the candidate and the party that can be taken into the remaining months of the campaign. Although there are other important functions, such as healing intraparty wounds (Campbell 1992, 288), these functions tend to further the objective of enhancing the candidate's and party's image before the electorate and improving the party's chances of victory in November.

The fact that the nomination is rarely in doubt before the convention does not mean that conventions are completely void of all zest and popular appeal. Contemporary conventions, as well orchestrated as they are, still generate substantial interest. Although there is less broadcast coverage of the conventions today than there used to be, upward of 70% of all households report watching some parts of the convention on television (Stanley and Niemi 1992, 76), and this figure does not even reflect the additional exposure that is generated through the print and radio media.

Nominating conventions in the contemporary era have left some lasting impressions on American politics. Sometimes these impressions are not what the candidates expected. The 1964 Republican convention, for instance, left us with Barry Goldwater's famous statement, ". . . extremism in the defense of liberty is no vice" (*Congressional Quarterly* 1987, 109). The 1968 Democratic convention left a lasting impression not so much for what went on in the convention hall as for the violence in the streets of Chicago. And, although it seemed to serve him well at the time, George Bush's most famous one-liner from the 1988 Republican convention, "Read my lips: no new taxes!," will no doubt go down in history as one of best examples of a good idea that came back to haunt the candidate four years later.

What is important for this analysis is that conventions provide the parties with a stage from which they can dominate not only news about the campaign but news in general for a period of several days. What is especially important to understand is that the conventions are held during a period when they are most likely to have an effect on public views toward the candidates. Although the candidates have been campaigning and may have been involved in tough primary battles, the general election campaign does not traditionally heat up until late summer. Given the relative paucity of information available, large doses of information such as those provided by the conventions are likely to carry more weight early in the campaign when voters have limited information and impressions are not well formed than later in the campaign when voters have been exposed to a large volume of information and are unlikely to learn as much from additional pieces of information.

Besides the fact that conventions offer the party an opportunity to present its candidate and image to the public, the party also has the opportunity to do this in a relatively uncontested format. Unlike the information in a presidential debate, which involves at least two candidates sharing the stage and challenging each other, the information generated by the convention is almost totally one-sided. Even if you allow for the occasional response by the opposing party on the evening news or media exposure of some problems within the party, the party has more control over the media message during the convention than during any other part of the campaign.

The importance of being able to dominate the flow of information during the convention period is not lost on the campaign strategists. On July 1, 1992, Stan Greenberg, the pollster for the Clinton campaign, issued a memo to "Bill Clinton and company" concerning the upcoming Democratic convention. In that memo Greenberg discussed the opportunity that the convention provided to the campaign:

> The convention period provides the only stage left in this election where we are alone—able to present Bill Clinton on his own terms. We were robbed of that stage in the late and post primary period by Ross Perot and thus dare not miss this opportunity. It will not come again. (Goldman, DeFrank, Miller, Murr, and Mathews 1994, 694)

The ability to dominate the flow of information is expected to work to the advantage of the party holding the convention, assuming that they are able to generate positive information. The anticipated consequence of the convention period is a "bump" in public support for the party holding the convention. As voters learn more about the candidate and are exposed to campaign rhetoric on behalf of the candidate, they are expected to be more likely to support the candidate, all else held equal. In the remainder of this chapter the magnitude and the origins of convention bumps are examined. The nominating conventions from 1984 to 1992 are given special attention in the following pages because they are more contemporary and because polling data are more abundant for these years than for earlier years. This is followed by a more general attempt to account for variation in the magnitude of convention bumps.

Nominating Conventions, 1984-1992

The six nominating conventions from 1984 to 1992 were held under a variety of circumstances. Some candidates were clear underdogs going into their convention whereas others held commanding leads. Some underdogs emerged from their conventions with leads whereas others continued to languish in the polls. Some conventions were divided and rife with issues, whereas others were very unified and uneventful. Thus, these six conventions provide a variety of experiences that should be useful for shedding light on the nature of the convention bump.

THE 1984 CONVENTIONS

The conventions of 1984 provide a nice example of what have come to be known as typical Democratic and Republican conventions. The Democratic convention period began on a positive note with the selection of Geraldine Ferraro as Walter Mondale's vice presidential running mate a week before the convention opened. The timing of this selection, along with the historical significance of selecting a woman, generated a lot of positive press and energized the Democratic party as it prepared for its convention. This was soon overshadowed, however, by signs of strife within the Democratic party. First, Mondale sought to have Charles Manatt removed as chair of the Democratic National Committee and replaced by Bert Lance, who had served as Jimmy Carter's budget director before resigning in the face of allegations of wrongdoing. The negative effects of this move were twofold. First, it created considerable dissension within the party, especially among those who supported Manatt. Manatt was very popular with many of the party leaders and was viewed as having done a good job putting the convention together. Just as Manatt was being toasted in San Francisco by many of the party's faithful, Mondale tried to replace him with a remnant of the Carter administration (Germond and Witcover 1985). Second, Mondale had "violated the cardinal rule of politics: Never step on your own good story" (Germond and Witcover 1985, 397). The disturbance created by the Manatt/Lance fiasco muted the potential for a positive response to the Ferraro selection. In the end, Mondale reversed himself and asked Manatt to stay on as chair of the party.

At the same time, there were problems brewing between Mondale and Jesse Jackson. When it became clear that Jackson was not being considered as a serious vice presidential candidate, his camp made noises about being ignored and hinted that Jewish leaders within the party had lobbied against his candidacy (Boyd 1984). In the end, Jackson made a moving speech before the convention in which he pledged to work hard for the ticket. Nevertheless, the signs of discord over both the Jackson and Manatt/Lance affairs dimmed the spotlight somewhat for the 1984 Democratic convention.

The 1984 Republican convention was a love-fest in comparison to the Democratic convention held a month earlier. The Republican ticket held a commanding lead in the polls and there were no signs of discord among the delegates gathered in Dallas to renominate the Reagan-Bush team. In fact, one concern voiced by the Reagan-Bush campaign was that there was so little real business to conduct that it might be hard to get people to watch the convention (Weisman, 1984). In the week prior to the convention, the dominant issue came not from within the Republican party but from the Democratic camp; questions about past taxes paid by Geraldine Ferraro and her husband, John Zaccaro, along with questions about his business dealings, stole the spotlight from the Republicans. Of course, this is the type of circumstance in which the Republicans were probably glad to relinquish some attention.

THE 1988 CONVENTIONS

The 1988 Democratic convention bore many similarities to the 1984 Democratic convention. First, the Dukakis campaign captured the media spotlight early by announcing the selection of Texas Senator Lloyd Bentsen as the vice presidential running mate a week before the convention. The selection of Bentsen was generally seen as a shrewd choice, bringing both geographic and ideological balance to the ticket. The euphoria over Bentsen's selection was short-lived, however. In the days following the selection of Bentsen, one of the major news stories focused on how the Dukakis campaign had failed to notify Jesse Jackson that he was not selected for the ticket. Instead, Jackson found out about the Bentsen selection when asked to comment on it by a reporter (Oreskes, 1988). Jackson's bruised feelings continued to be an important aspect of the convention although the two candidates apparently patched things up and Jackson endorsed the ticket when he addressed the convention.

One significant way in which the 1988 Democratic convention differed from the 1984 convention was that the ticket went into the convention with a lead in the polls and a sense of optimism concerning the fall campaign. This sense of optimism set the tone for the convention, which featured raucous speeches from the likes of Texas governor Ann Richards ("Poor George. He can't help it. He was born with a silver foot in his mouth.") and Massachusetts Senator Edward Kennedy ("Where was George?").

The 1988 Republican convention represented the end of the Reagan era and the passing of the torch to Vice President George Bush. The most prominent issue for this convention was the vice presidential nomination, which was not announced until the opening day of the convention. George Bush's selection of Dan Quayle as his running mate took the convention by surprise and created problems for the Republicans. Almost immediately there were questions about Quayle's qualifications and about his past; in particular there were questions about whether Quayle had received preferential treatment to help him get into the National Guard so he could avoid being drafted during the Vietnam War. Besides presenting problems for the party because they raised doubts about Quayle's qualifications, these issues were also troubling for the Republicans because they were a significant distraction from the reason why the delegates had gathered in New Orleans: to nominate George Bush and make a case for his candidacy to the American people.

Other than the problems created by the Quayle nomination, the 1988 Republican convention came off without a hitch. Ronald Reagan gave a sentimental speech in which he wholeheartedly endorsed Bush and answered, " 'George was there' " (Runkel 1989, 289). George Bush ended the convention with a strong acceptance speech in which he defended his running mate, promised a kinder and gentler nation, and made his infamous "no new taxes" pledge.

THE 1992 CONVENTIONS

The 1992 conventions represented a departure from the previous two election years: The Democrats had a relatively unified and well-orchestrated convention whereas there were signs of distress on the Republican side. The Democratic convention got off to a good start during the week prior to the convention with the announcement of Senator Albert Gore of Tennessee as Clinton's choice for a vice presidential running mate. Gore's selection was generally viewed as a solid addition to the Democratic ticket and generated a lot of enthusiasm among the Democrats as they went into the their convention. At the same time, Clinton was moving ahead in the polls and Ross Perot's campaign was experiencing difficulties. The Clinton campaign received the ultimate windfall when Perot announced on the last day of the Democratic convention that he was quitting the race. To cap things off for the Democrats, Perot said that part of the reason he was getting out of the race was the "revitalization of the Democratic party" (Goldman et al. 1994, 478).

The convention itself was relatively uneventful by Democratic standards. Divisiveness within the party, such as Jerry Brown's opposition to Clinton and the refusal to allow Pennsylvania governor Robert Casey, who is prolife, to speak before the convention, was downplayed and did not dominate the convention news. One of the highlights of the convention was the presentation of a Hollywood-produced film about the life of Bill Clinton, beginning with his childhood in Hope, Arkansas. In this film and throughout the convention period, Bill Clinton was seemingly transformed from a candidate with a lot of problems to "a man from Hope."

The Gore and Clinton acceptance speeches were well received and the Democrats left their convention on a positive note. Following the convention, the Clinton-Gore team tried to keep the momentum going by embarking on a bus trip through several states that received widespread press coverage.

The 1992 Republican convention was held under a cloud—the cloud of dismal poll results and intraparty squabbling. Most polls at the time showed Clinton with a commanding and seemingly insurmountable lead. In addition, in the weeks prior to the convention, there was public squabbling among party members over whether to dump Dan Quayle from the ticket. The talk of dumping Quayle had become so widespread that even Gerald Ford had let it be known that he thought Quayle should be replaced (Goldman et al. 1994, 380). In an effort to jump-start the campaign, Secretary of State James Baker left the State Department to join the campaign staff, although his official title was Chief of Staff and Chief Counselor to the President.

Prior to the convention, the specter of divisiveness over the issue of abortion also reared its ugly head. This was brought on by statements made by Vice President Quayle and President Bush in which they reported that if a daughter or granddaughter were pregnant and thinking about abortion they would discourage her but that, ultimately, the decision should be left to her. These statements were followed a few days later by Barbara Bush's admonition that abortion should not be addressed by either party's platform (Apple, 1992). The Republican convention did not focus exclusively on the abortion issue but did emphasize the importance of values and attacked the record of both Bill Clinton and his wife, Hillary. Many of the attacks on the Clintons may have backfired, however, due to their personal and sharply negative tone. In the end, both Vice President Quayle and President Bush made well-received acceptance speeches and the delegates left the convention feeling better about the race than they had at the beginning of the convention.

Given the differences in the circumstances of these six conventions, it should be expected that the conventions had different effects on public support for the candidates. Presumably, the convention environment has an effect on the message the convention conveys to the electorate, which in turn should have an effect on how the public responds to the conventions. In the next section, evidence is brought to bear on these and other issues.

The Electoral Payoff

One of the expected benefits of the quadrennial party nominating conventions is a boost in the polls, or what has come to be known as a convention "bump." In theory, because the party has had an opportunity to present its ticket in a favorable light the level of public support for the ticket should be higher after the convention than before the convention. Campbell, Cherry, and Wink studied convention bumps from 1964 to 1988 and found that "in most cases conventions continue to fulfill the 'rally function' for political parties" (1992, 302). According to Campbell et al., the typical convention bump is between a 5 and 7 percentage point increase in the polls.

The magnitude and genesis of the convention bump are examined in the remainder of this chapter. First, the effect of the conventions on public support for the candidates from 1984 to 1992 is examined in some detail. This is followed by an analysis of the role played by information in creating these convention effects. Finally, an information-based model is offered to explain the variation in convention "bumps" from 1964 to 1992.

CONVENTION BUMPS: 1984-1992

The measurement of convention effects is relatively straightforward. The expectation is that due to the type and amount of information generated by

the convention, an aggregate shift in candidate support favoring the convening party's candidate will occur following the convention. To detect these
effects it is necessary to measure the level of candidate support before and
after the convention. Presumably, there will be a significant difference
between the two periods. Figure 4.1 illustrates the flow of candidate support
from early June to election day during 1984, 1988, and 1992 campaigns, and
highlights the point at which each of the party conventions occurred.[1] The
left axis of this figure displays the Republican percentage point advantage
(Republican percentage minus Democratic percentage) over the Democratic
candidate: Negative values indicate a net Democratic advantage and positive
values indicate a net Republican advantage. The timeline of the campaign is
displayed on the horizontal axis.

Several important patterns emerge from Figure 4.1. First, each campaign
appears to have its own unique dynamic. In 1984, candidate support mean-
dered back and forth but never strayed into a danger zone for the Reagan
campaign. The greatest threat to the Reagan campaign occurred in the
aftermath of the Democratic convention, when the Reagan advantage slipped
to below 8 percentage points. In 1988 and 1992, however, there was a pattern
that can best be described as a "reversal of fortune": The leading candidate
prior to the convention period came out as the trailing candidate in the postconvention period. Also, each of the six conventions appears to be associated
with a shift in candidate support in favor of the party holding the convention.
In many cases, such as the 1988 Republican convention and the 1984 and
1992 Democratic conventions, the shift in support appears to begin at some
point prior to the opening of the convention, perhaps reflecting the effect of
publicity given to preconvention activities such as the vice presidential
selection process. Finally, the magnitude of the convention bump appears to
vary a great deal across the six conventions. Again, the 1988 and 1992
conventions appear to have altered the course of the campaign whereas the
1984 conventions do not appear to be associated with such large-scale
changes.

Table 4.1 documents the magnitude of the convention bumps displayed in
Figure 4.1. The method used to calculate the convention bumps is borrowed
from Campbell et al. (1992). The level of support before the convention is
based on trial-heat polls taken between six days and two weeks prior to the
opening of the convention. The level of support for the postconvention
period is based on trial heat polls taken during the week following the last

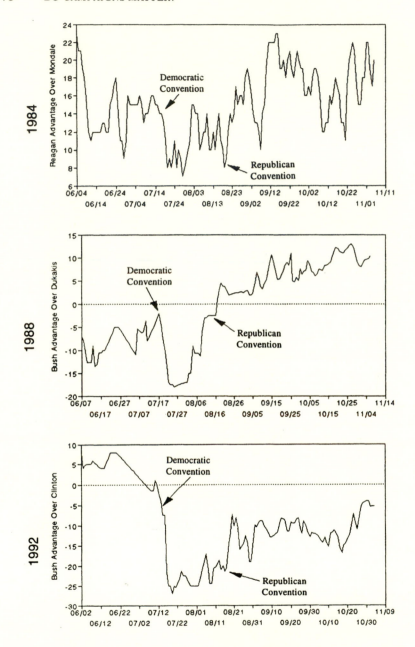

Figure 4.1. The Electoral Impact of Conventions, 1984-1992

Table 4.1   Convention Bumps, 1984-1992

Year	Party	Before	After	Bump
1984	Democratic	41.9%	45.3%	+3.4
	Republican	56.2%	58.7%	+2.5
1988	Democratic	53.6%	60.4%	+6.8
	Republican	43.5%	51.9%	+8.4
1992	Democratic	50.8%	64.4%	+13.6
	Republican	38.6%	43.0%	+4.4

NOTE: All entries are based on a comparison of polls taken from six days to two weeks prior to each convention with those taken during the week following the convention. The percentages are based on the number of respondents supporting one of the two major party candidates.

day of the convention. The percentages are based on the candidate's share of respondents who supported one of the two major party candidates and the convention bump is the difference between the postconvention vote share and the preconvention vote share. Measured in this way, the convention bumps presented in Table 4.1 represent the short-term increase in candidate support for the convening party's candidate.[2]

Two clear findings emerge from Table 4.1. First, there are significant changes in candidate support following the conventions and second, there is significant variation in the magnitude of convention bumps from 1984 to 1992. The smallest convention effects are found in the 1984 conventions (2.5 and 3.4 points) and the 1992 Republican convention (4.4 points). The largest convention bump was generated by the 1992 Democratic convention (13.6 points), followed by the 1988 Republican convention (8.4 points) and the 1988 Democratic convention (6.8 points).

Documenting the magnitude of convention bumps is the easy part of this analysis. A much more daunting task is to explain the process that produces these effects and to attempt to explain differences in the magnitude of the convention bumps. To that task we now turn.

Information and Convention Bumps

The first expectation is that the amount and nature of information produced during the convention period is responsible for the generation of postconvention bumps in candidate support. Recall from Chapter 3 that nominating conventions were found to be associated with significant spikes in the total amount of campaign information generated by the media. The primary focus of campaign coverage generated during the convention period is assumed to be on the party holding the convention, and this ability to dominate the news is assumed to contribute to the convention bump. The analysis in Chapter 3, however, focused on the total amount of campaign coverage without regard to which side was being covered. Although it is expected that the information spikes during the convention periods result from increased coverage of the activities of the convening party, it is also possible that some of this coverage is dedicated to counterconvention activities of the other party. To get a clearer picture of the degree to which the convening party is able to dominate the news, the pattern of press coverage during the campaign, broken down by candidate, is presented in Figure 4.2. Specifically, Figure 4.2 presents the average daily number of paragraphs about each of the candidates for week-long intervals beginning June first and continuing through election day.[3] These graphs make it possible to discern not only how much information is being generated by the conventions but also the degree to which the party holding the convention is able to dominate the news during the convention period.

There are some very clear similarities in the flow of information across the three campaigns. First, each campaign is able to dominate the news during the period of its party's convention. This is more so the case in some convention periods than others, but both parties are generally able to dominate the flow of campaign communications during their convention. Second, the Democratic conventions tend to produce slightly larger spikes in information than do the Republican conventions. This may reflect the fact that the Democratic conventions are held earlier in these three years and involve nonincumbent candidates about whom there is more to learn. Alternatively, this finding might reflect the fact that the Democratic conventions are usually more spirited and provide the media with more opportunities for "eventful" coverage. Third, although each campaign is able to dominate the news during its convention period, there is no clear pattern of news dominance in the period between the last convention and election day. Instead, both candidates receive roughly the same amount of coverage from week to week in the weeks following the conventions. This highlights the importance of conventions: They represent the only time during the campaign when the parties are able to exercise clear control over the flow of campaign information.

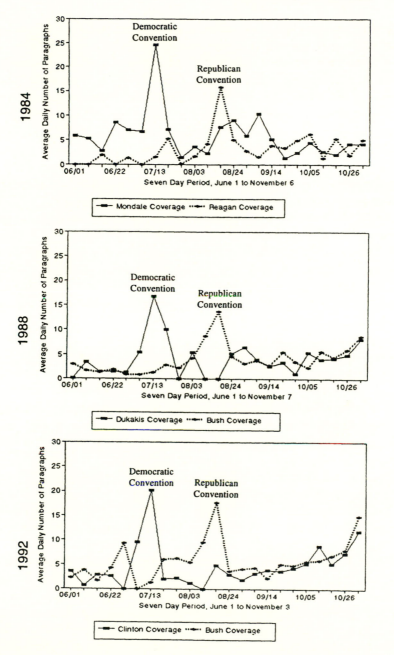

Figure 4.2. Total Front-Page *New York Times* Campaign Coverage, by Candidate, 1984-1992

Although the data in Figure 4.2 are very supportive of the hypothesis that the convention bump emanates from the information advantage afforded to the convening party, the magnitude of the information "bump" does not appear to bear a strong relationship to the magnitude of the electoral bump associated with the conventions. The 1984 Democratic convention generated far more front-page coverage than any of the other five conventions held from 1984 to 1992 yet the 1984 Democratic convention produced one of the smallest electoral bumps (3.4 points) of this period. There are other anomalies in Figure 4.2 that cloud the relationship between media exposure and the size of the convention bump. For instance, in 1988 the Democratic campaign drew more press coverage during their convention than the Republicans did but the Republicans received a substantially larger electoral bump from their convention (8.4 points versus 6.8 points).

Events such as conventions are supposed to afford the campaigns an opportunity to provide important information to the electorate—information that will enhance the candidate's standing in the polls. The patterns of campaign communications presented in Figure 4.2 are only partially supportive of this hypothesis: Campaigns do receive substantial increases in media exposure during their convention period, increases that more than likely produce postconvention bumps in candidate support. However, the relative level of exposure is not strongly related to the magnitude of the convention bumps. One possible explanation for this is that all information is not created equally or, to put it another way, more information is not always a good thing. Generally speaking, increased media exposure is good for a campaign only if the content of the exposure is positive. Grabbing the media spotlight hardly does a campaign any good if the focus of that spotlight is on negative aspects of the campaign. Instead, campaigns can only be expected to benefit from an information flow that is positive in nature.

Consider the dominant news items immediately prior to and during the six conventions under study here. Recall that the positive publicity generated by the Ferraro nomination in 1984 was knocked off the front page by Mondale's botched attempt to replace Charles Manatt with Bert Lance as chair of the Democratic party and by a rift between Mondale and Jesse Jackson. These are clearly not positive news stories but they are stories that received a lot of coverage. Even though the Democrats got more coverage from the 1984 convention than any of the other conventions, the coverage was not all positive. Also, the 1984 Republicans had a harder time dominating the media during their convention than any of the other convention during this period.

In fact, coverage of the Democratic campaign actually increased significantly during the Republican convention period. However, this increase in
Democratic coverage did not necessarily hurt the Republicans because the
biggest story in the week prior to the 1984 Republican convention was the
potential tax problems involving Geraldine Ferraro and her husband John
Zaccaro. The point here is that the quantity of coverage is perhaps not all
that matters; the quality of coverage may be just as important. As described
earlier, some conventions are held in a relatively tranquil, scandal-free
environment, whereas others are more divisive and provide more opportunities for negative press coverage. Given the diversity of circumstances surrounding the conventions, it is perhaps necessary to focus on the tone of press
coverage rather than just on the sheer quantity of coverage.

In an effort to measure the tone of press coverage, the same news coverage
presented in Figure 4.2 is analyzed for content. Specifically, each front-page
campaign story is evaluated on the basis of which campaign or candidate is
the subject of the story and whether the story is negative or nonnegative in
nature. Negative stories are those that point to problems in the campaign or
within the party, scandal or potential scandal, unfavorable poll standing, or
direct criticism of the candidate or someone affiliated with the campaign. All
other stories are judged to be nonnegative in nature. Rather than try to make
the difficult distinction between neutral and positive coverage, it was decided
that all nonnegative coverage is of benefit to the campaign and therefore can
be considered positive. Once a story was classified by candidate and tone,
the total number of paragraphs in the story were tallied as negative or
nonnegative paragraphs, depending on the tone of the story.[4]

To measure the tone of coverage for a candidate, all negative paragraphs
are assigned a value of −1, all nonnegative paragraphs are assigned a value
of +1, and the value of all paragraphs is then summed together, yielding a
variable that takes into account both the quantity *and* the quality of press
coverage for the candidate over a given period of time. Of course, one
candidate's positive press coverage should not only help that candidate but
should also hurt the opposing candidate. Therefore, it is useful to think of
press coverage in terms of the net tone, or the balance of the tone of coverage
for both candidates. Suppose, for instance, that on a hypothetical day the tone
of coverage for the Republican candidate is equal to a value of +10 and the
tone of coverage for the Democratic candidate is equal to a value of +6. In
this case the net tone of the coverage for the Republican candidate is equal
to +4, which is the value of the coverage for the Republican candidate minus

the value of the coverage for the Democratic candidate. Conversely, the net tone for the Democratic candidate is equal to –4.

The concept of tone of press coverage is essential to an understanding of how information can affect public opinion during a presidential campaign. Using the concept of net tone, it is possible not only to control for the volume and type of information that is being generated about a candidate but also to control for the same characteristics about information concerning opposing candidates. Figure 4.3 presents the average daily net tone of campaign coverage for weeklong periods from June 1 through the election in 1984, 1988, and 1992. Specifically, the vertical axis represents the net tone for the Republican candidates—that is, the tone of coverage for the Republican candidate minus the tone of coverage for the Democratic candidate. Negative values on the vertical axis indicate a tonal deficit for the Republican candidate, or a Democratic advantage in press coverage. Positive values indicate a tonal surplus, or a Republican advantage in press coverage.

Conventions appear to have a similar effect on press coverage across the three election years. In each year there are substantial increases in positive coverage for the Democratic campaign (negative Republican tone) during the period of the Democratic convention and significant increases in positive coverage of the Republican campaign during the period of the Republican convention. In some cases, such as both conventions in 1984 and the 1992 Democratic convention, the change in press tone is especially apparent. In other cases, such as the 1992 Republican convention, the change in coverage is not nearly as noticeable. In the period between the last convention and election day, there appears to be a slight Republican advantage in press coverage in 1984, a more pronounced Republican advantage in 1988, and a meandering pattern to press coverage in 1992.

More precise estimates of the effect of conventions on press coverage are summarized in Table 4.2, which presents a regression analysis of the effect of conventions on the tone of press coverage. The dependent variable in this analysis is the net tone of press coverage. Unlike the data in Figure 4.3, however, the data analyzed in Table 4.2 are daily readings of press tone. The model includes three independent variables: a lagged variable representing the tone of coverage on the previous day, and dummy variables for each of the two conventions, coded 1 for the period from four days before to four days after the conventions are held and coded 0 for all other days. The regression results confirm what appeared to be the case from a visual inspection of the data: The conventions do, usually, generate significantly

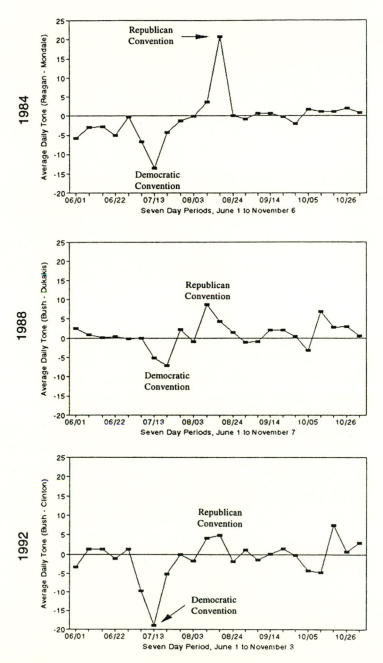

Figure 4.3. Net Tone of Front-Page *New York Times* Campaign Coverage, 1984-1992

Table 4.2   The Impact of Nominating Conventions on the Daily Tone of
Front-Page *New York Times* Coverage of the Campaign, 1984-1992
(OLS Results)

	1984 b	1988 b	1992 b
Constant	−.71	.86*	−.40
	(.74)	(.57)	(.68)
Net press tone $(t-1)$	.16*	.15*	.09
	(.082)	(.08)	(1.15)
Democratic convention	−10.47**	−5.41**	−13.58**
	(2.92)	(2.12)	(2.66)
Republican convention	13.07**	4.62**	4.04*
	(3.00)	(2.14)	(2.39)
N	158	159	154
R^2	.29	.13	.24
Durbin-Watson	1.97	2.04	2.00

NOTE: Standard errors are in parentheses.
$*p < .10$; $**p < .05$.

more positive news about the candidate's campaign than is produced during
the rest of the campaign period. The one exception to this is the 1992
Republican convention, for which there was only a marginally significant
increase in the level of positive press given to the Bush campaign. Although
the Bush campaign received a boost in the amount of coverage during the
convention period (see Figure 4.2), the tone of this coverage was not
altogether favorable. Many of the stories during this period focused on
Bush's vulnerability in the polls and strife within the Republican party.
Overall, the weight of these negative stories was enough to rob the Bush
campaign of all but a barely discernible increase in the tone of coverage.

The correspondence between the occurrence of conventions and the
change in press tone goes a long way toward explaining the source of
convention bumps: Candidates are able to use the convention to generate a
positive message that results in an increase in public support. However,
although the changes in the tone of press coverage during the convention
period might help explain the existence of conventions bumps, they are of
only marginal use in explaining variation in the magnitude of the convention

bump across conventions. To some extent the differences in tone of coverage do correspond with the differences in the size of the convention bump. For instance, in 1992 the Democrats received substantially better coverage during their convention than the Republicans did one month later, and they also received a substantially large postconvention electoral bump (+13.6 points versus +4.4 points). The picture becomes a bit murkier, however, when looking at the other years. For example, the 1984 Republican convention saw a favorable increase in press coverage nearly equal to that of the 1992 Democratic convention, but the convention bump for the 1984 Republican convention (+2.5) is smaller than any of the other five conventions listed in Table 4.1. In general, there is only a weak relationship between the change in the tone of press coverage and the magnitude of the convention bump. This does not mean that press tone is not related to convention bumps, only that the differences in the magnitude of convention bumps is not easily explained by the magnitude of the changes in the tone of press coverage during the convention period.

Part of the explanation of the modest relationship between press tone and the magnitude of the convention bump lies in the fact that there are limits on the ability of information, no matter how positive or negative, to have an effect on aggregate opinion. In particular, there are certain points during a campaign when information is likely to have a greater effect. Based on the hypotheses developed in Chapter 3, campaign information is expected to have a greater effect on public opinion when information is scarce and when public opinion is significantly out of equilibrium. In the next section, an effort is made to ascertain the role of these two factors in determining the effect of conventions on public opinion.

Explaining Convention Bumps, 1964-1992

An exhaustive analysis of how scarcity of information and opinion disequilibrium influence the magnitude of convention bumps is not possible, using just the six conventions from 1984 to 1992. Instead, it is necessary to expand the analysis to include other years and other conventions. For this purpose, the analysis now shifts to explaining differences in convention bumps from 1964 to 1992. Estimates of these bumps are presented in Figure 4.4, from which several observations can be made.[5] First, nearly every convention from 1964 to 1992 resulted in a positive bump in public support

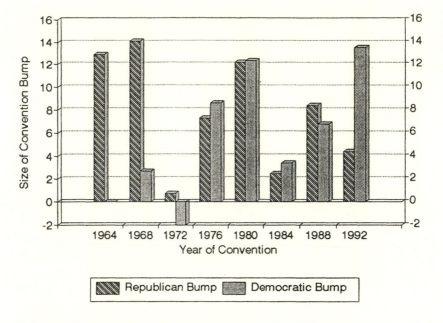

Figure 4.4. Convention Bumps, 1964-1992

for the ticket of the convening party. The two exceptions to this are the Democratic conventions of 1964 and 1972: In 1964, the Democrats were in the same position coming out of the convention as they were going into the convention (no bump), and in 1972 the Democrats were actually 2 percentage points lower in the polls following the convention than before the convention. Second, in many cases there are relatively modest convention bumps: For the Republican conventions of 1972, 1984, and 1992, and the Democratic conventions of 1968 and 1984, the convention bumps were less than 5 percentage points. Finally, for the remaining conventions the postconvention bumps are quite substantial, climbing as high as 14.1 percentage points for the Republicans in 1968.

How can the differences in the magnitude of these sixteen convention bumps be explained? In particular, how can the hypotheses regarding the role of information and equilibrium be used to explain these differences? One approach that is sometimes tempting is to closely examine the individual circumstances of each convention. After all, as described earlier in this chapter, each convention occurs in a somewhat different context. The problem with this approach is that it will ultimately yield sixteen separate explanations—one for each convention. Instead, this analysis attempts a more general approach to explaining the pattern found in Figure 4.4, an approach based on the expected effect of information generated during the convention period.

TIMING IS EVERYTHING

Campbell et al. (1992) found that the first convention of the season usually generates a larger bump than the second convention of the season. Campbell et al. offered two possible explanations for this difference, both of which are related to the usefulness of the information generated by the convention. First, because the first convention occurs early in the general election season, a larger proportion of the electorate may be undecided and may be more susceptible to the influence of campaign information. No doubt this creates a situation in which there are more opportunities for persuasion during the first convention than during the second. However, in addition to more voters being undecided, it must be remembered that voters in general are in possession of less campaign information at this point in the process than they are during the second convention period. This is not to suggest that there is no information available to voters prior to the convention. Indeed, a heated primary season can generate a lot of information about the candidates, albeit for a much smaller audience. Although some voters may have paid attention to the primary campaign and there is some degree of postprimary/preconvention campaigning, the first convention provides a substantial burst of campaign information onto a relatively barren information landscape (see Figure 4.2). Because of the relative scarcity of campaign information prior to the first convention, the value (to the consumer) of the information generated by the convention is likely to be quite high. To be sure, the second convention also generates a significant amount of information, which is why the second convention also produces a convention bump. However, the marginal value of each additional piece of information generated by the second convention is likely to be less than that produced by the first convention, because of the *relative* abundance of information available to voters prior to the second convention.

The information generated by the first convention is also likely to be of greater value to voters because, traditionally, the challenging party holds its convention first (Campbell et al. 1992, 298). Because the challenging party holds its convention first, voters are likely to have less information about the presidential and vice presidential nominees and there is likely to be greater demand for information during this convention than during the second or incumbent party convention. Again, this does not mean voters have no information about the out-party candidate, only that there is more to be learned about the out-party candidate than there is about the incumbent party candidate. This difference in demand for information exacerbates the difference in the value and therefore the expected effect of the information generated by the conventions. Consider the 1992 conventions as an example. The Democrats nominated Bill Clinton, governor of a relatively small state, Arkansas. Although Clinton, as governor, had been actively involved in national politics, most Americans had little exposure to Bill Clinton the presidential candidate. To the extent that most Americans had any information about Clinton, it was probably based on some of the more sensational stories about personal issues that came out of the primary season. By early summer there was still a lot that the public could learn about Clinton and the convention provided the classroom where that learning could take place. Now consider the 1992 Republican convention. The Republicans nominated George Bush, the incumbent Republican president and Dan Quayle, the incumbent vice president. Bush had been president for almost four years and had been vice president for eight years. What were the Republicans going to tell the American public about Bush that they did not already know or think they knew? Certainly, the Republicans had a much smaller opportunity to "educate" the public concerning their candidate in 1992 than did the Democrats. This pattern holds throughout the period analyzed here: From 1964 to 1992, the challenging party always held its convention first and the incumbent party always nominated a sitting president or vice president.

The first convention, then, affords the party a good opportunity to effectively transmit its message for three reasons: There is a large pool of undecided voters who need information to make their voting decision, information is relatively scarce at this point in the campaign, and the voters generally have less information about the challenging party, which is the first to hold its convention. All of this creates a situation in which information is much more valuable to the public during the first convention than during the second.

EQUILIBRIUM BALANCE

One of the hypotheses advanced in Chapter 3 suggested that there is an equilibrium, or expected level of candidate support, during each of the campaign seasons and that the potential effect of any campaign event is partially dependent on the degree to which public opinion is out of equilibrium. If candidate support is far below the expected level, then a positive event has greater potential for boosting the candidate's standing than if candidate support is near or exceeding the expected level of support. If candidate support is near to or exceeds the equilibrium level, then there is a smaller portion of the public available that is likely to be persuaded by campaign communications. It is easy to see how this logic can be used to explain differences in the size of convention bumps. Consider the conventions of 1964, 1972, and 1984, for instance. In 1964, the preconvention polls showed the Republican candidate with 21% of the vote and the Democratic candidate with 69% of the vote. The expected vote, based on the spring forecasting model developed in Chapter 2, is 39% for the Republican candidate and 61% for the Democratic candidate. The difference between the level of preconvention support and the expected level of support, what might be termed the *equilibrium deficit,* was –18 percentage points for the Republicans and +8 percentage points for the Democrats. Is it any wonder that the Republicans gained almost 13 percentage points as a result of their convention, whereas the Democrats managed only to hold even? The Republicans had a lot of room for improvement and the Democrats were already running better than they should have been. Likewise, in 1972 both parties were running ahead of where they should have been prior to their conventions: The Democrats were 3.4 points ahead of their expected level and the Republicans were 2.7 points ahead. Given this, it makes sense that neither party significantly improved its standing in the postconvention period (the Republican bump was +0.7 and the Democratic "bump" was –2.0), although it is still unusual that the Democrats actually lost support.

In addition, one possible reason that the 1984 conventions produced relatively small bumps despite their substantial effect on positive press coverage (see Table 4.2 and Figure 4.3) is that both parties were very near their expected level of support going into the conventions. In cases such as these, where there is not much room for improvement in the polls, it is less likely that events such as conventions will substantially alter the relative standing of the candidates.

THE CONVENTION ENVIRONMENT

In addition to the timing of the convention and preconvention equilibrium deficit, it is important to consider what actually happens at the convention. The discussion earlier in this chapter suggested that the circumstances of the convention and the activities of the convention have an effect on the type of news coverage and, therefore, the effect of the convention on public opinion, all else held equal. The difficulty, however, lies in determining exactly which convention circumstances are likely to yield the greatest gains. Campbell et al. (1992) suggest that relatively unified conventions that had been preceded by divided nomination contests provide the best opportunity for parties to advance their cause. Evidence supporting this relationship, as reported by Campbell et al., is weak, however.

Although almost any method of classifying conventions as "good" or "bad" is likely to have a large arbitrary component and will be post hoc in nature, some conventions are more easily labeled than others. During the period under discussion here, for instance, the 1968 and 1972 Democratic conventions stand out as particularly disastrous for the convening party. Both conventions were divisive and both were saddled with problems that tarnished the image of the party and its candidate. In 1968 the media were distracted by the violence and unrest on the streets of Chicago that occurred at the same time as the convention. Attention was focused on the problems in the streets of Chicago rather than on the nomination of Hubert Humphrey. Even when the media focused on the convention itself, it usually found near-riot conditions inside the convention hall. In 1972, a divided vice presidential roll call pushed George McGovern's acceptance speech back to nearly three o'clock in the morning, when most of the potential audience was fast asleep (*Congressional Quarterly* 1987, 120), thereby effectively robbing the nominee of the most important opportunity he would have to convey his message to the American people. There can be little question but that circumstances such as these hinder a party's ability to translate the convention period into a significant increase in candidate support. Of course, although other conventions (the Republican conventions of 1976 and 1992, and the 1980 Democratic convention, for instance) may not have gone as well as the nominees would have liked, there can be little doubt that the 1968 and 1972 Democratic conventions provide the clearest examples of conventions gone awry.

Table 4.3   Determinants of Convention Bumps, 1964-1992 (OLS Results)

	b	b
Intercept	3.73**	2.88
	(1.37)	(1.73)
Democrats, 1968 and 1972	−7.93**	—
	(2.56)	—
Equilibrium balance	−.39**	−.36**
	(.12)	(.15)
First convention	5.65**	5.54**
	(1.77)	(2.28)
N	16	16
R^2	0.67	0.41
Adjusted R^2	0.59	0.32

NOTE: Standard errors are in parentheses.
**$p < .05$.

ANALYSIS OF CONVENTION BUMPS

A regression model of convention bumps from 1964 to 1992 is presented in Table 4.3 and includes operational variables that capture the type of effects previously discussed. The dependent variable in this analysis is the magnitude of convention bumps from 1964 to 1992, as displayed in Figure 4.4, yielding 16 observations. Due to the small number of observations it is necessary to include as few independent variables as possible. First, there is a dummy variable to control for the unique circumstances of the 1968 and 1972 Democratic conventions. This variable is scored 1 for the 1968 and 1972 Democratic conventions and 0 for all other conventions. The expectation is that the coefficient for this variable will be negative, reflecting the poor performance of the Democrats in these conventions.

Second, a variable is included to measure the equilibrium balance in the period prior to the convention. This variable was created by subtracting the expected level of party support (as predicted by the spring forecasting model in Table 2.2) from the preconvention level of support for the party in public opinion polls (see Table 4.2 and Campbell et al. 1992). The difference between the expected and preconvention levels of support reflects the potential for increasing candidate support during the convention period. The larger the negative disparity between the expected and actual levels of support, the greater the potential for improvement. If the two numbers are relatively close or if the preconvention levels of support is higher than expected, then there is less room for improvement in the polls. Therefore, the coefficient for the equilibrium balance variable is expected to be negative.

Third, a dummy variable is added to control for the effect of being the first party to hold a convention. This variable is scored 1 for the earlier convention and 0 for the second convention. Based on the previous discussion of this variable, it is expected that candidates will receive a larger electoral bump from the first convention than from the second. Therefore, it is anticipated that the coefficient for this variable will be positive.

The first column of Table 4.3 presents the OLS regression analysis of convention bumps. These results provide strong support for the hypothesized effects. First, there is a significant negative relationship between equilibrium balance and the size of the convention bump. For every percentage point disparity between the expected level of support and the actual preconvention level of support, the convention bump is reduced by .39 percentage points. Because the coefficient is negative, preconvention deficits in support (lower than expected) translate into large convention bumps. For instance, in 1964 Goldwater was 18.3 percentage points below his equilibrium level of support in the preconvention polls. This preconvention deficit accounts for 7.1 points (the product of the deficit, −18.3, times the coefficient −.39) of his 12.9-point convention bump. Had Goldwater not been running such a support deficit he would not have seen nearly as large a convention bump.

Holding the first convention also has the anticipated effect on the convention bump. The party that holds the first convention has an expected convention bump that is 5.65 points higher than the bump garnered by the party holding the second convention, all else held equal. It is difficult to tell how much of this effect is due to holding the convention early in the season when information is scarce, versus how much of it is due to the fact that the second convention frequently (6 out 8 times) renominates an incumbent president about whom people already have a lot of information. Both factors are probably at work here.

Second, as anticipated, the Democrats did worse in 1968 and 1972 than expected, based on the other variables in the model. According to this coefficient, the Democrats should have had convention bumps almost eight points higher than they actually did have in 1968 and 1972. Although this effect probably did not matter much to the overall outcome of the 1972 election, it may have been very important in 1968 when the election outcome was very close and every vote was important. One could argue that this variable is simply controlling for the outlier status of these two conventions and may be biasing the estimates for the other variables. As a check on this possibility, the model was analyzed again without the inclusion of the control variable for the 1968 and 1972 Democratic conventions. The results of this analysis (second column, Table 4.3) show that the coefficients for the other variables are relatively unaffected by the inclusion (or exclusion) of the 1968 and 1972 Democratic dummy variable.[6]

The three variables analyzed in Table 4.3 are all significant and the coefficients are in the anticipated direction. As a group, these variables are also able to account for much of the variation in convention bumps (adjusted R^2 = .59). In general, the model provides fairly accurate estimates of the convention bumps: The mean absolute error of the model is 2.61 percentage points. In two cases (the 1964 and 1988 Democratic conventions) the estimated bumps were less than 1 percentage point different from the actual bump. The most egregious error is found in the estimate for the 1984 Democratic convention that predicted a bump (8.96) that was 5.56 points higher than the actual bump (3.40). Discrepancies such as this may point to events surrounding the convention, such as the Manatt/Lance shake-up, that can cause the candidate to gain more or less than expected. On average, however, this sort of event caused relatively small deviations from the expected size of the convention bumps.

Conclusion

Generally speaking, candidates can expect a bump in public support following their party's nominating convention. The origin of this bump lies in the ability of the campaign to dominate the media and to receive generally positive coverage during the campaign period. The analysis in this chapter found that press coverage generally does take on a net positive tone for the convening party (Figure 4.3). By providing the party with a relatively uncontested stage on which to present their candidate, the conventions provide a rare opportunity for the campaigns to reach voters. In most cases, this opportunity translates into positive movement in the polls.

But some conventions clearly generate more movement than others; some bumps are substantial, whereas others are modest. In particular, the party holding the first convention traditionally experiences a larger postconvention surge than the party holding the second convention. Part of the explanation for this is that the information provided by the first convention is of more value to voters because political information is more scarce early in the process and most voters have relatively little information about the nominee from the challenging party, which holds its convention first. The quality of the message conveyed by the convention can also have an effect on the popular response to the convention. The 1968 and 1972 Democratic conventions, for instance, were fraught with problems and generated convention bumps substantially smaller than expected.

However, there are real limits to the potential effect of conventions on public opinion. First, the effect of conventions is limited by the potential for improvement in the polls—what is referred to here as equilibrium balance. If a candidate is doing better than expected in the preconvention polls, then there is little room for improvement and the convention bump is likely to be modest. On the other hand, if a candidate is doing substantially worse than expected in the preconvention polls, there is a larger reservoir of untapped support waiting to be activated and the convention bump is likely to be of a larger magnitude. The second limitation on convention effects has to do not with the magnitude of the bump but with the potential for influencing the election outcome. Large convention bumps in some years are not necessarily more important to the eventual outcome than smaller bumps in other years. In 1964, for instance, Goldwater was the benefactor of a +12.9-point convention bump but he still never threatened Johnson. Also, in 1980, Jimmy Carter received a +12.4-point convention bump but this was still not enough for him to overcome Reagan. Clearly in some years the convention bumps appear to play a pivotal role, but it must be remembered that even a large convention bump does not necessarily change the face of the campaign.

Notes

1. The data in this figure are the same as those presented in Figure 3.6 and described in the appendix.

2. An alternative means of measuring the convention bump would be to compare the pre- and postconvention level of support for a longer period of time, perhaps even over the course of the campaign. For instance, one might divide the campaign into three periods—the pre-Democratic convention period, the interconvention period, and post-Republican convention period—and compare levels of candidate support across these periods. The problem with a long-term measure of convention effects such as this one is that it is likely to be confounded by the occurrence of other important events during the campaign. In the absence of control variables for other events, it is safer to use a short-term measure of convention bumps such as the one used in Table 4.1. This

measure has the added advantage of making the results comparable to those generated by Campbell et al. (1992) for other elections, which will be used later in this chapter.

3. Candidate paragraphs are defined as paragraphs from stories that have as their subject the candidate, the candidate's party, or someone affiliated with the candidate or party in a manner related to the campaign. Again, as mentioned in Chapter 3, references to noncampaign activities on the part of incumbent presidents and vice presidents are not included in the paragraph count.

4. Some stories were about the campaign in general, which means both campaigns were the subject of the story. In cases such as this, when the story did not clearly favor one campaign over the other the number of paragraphs were split between the campaigns.

5. The convention bumps from 1984 to 1992 are the same as those reported in Table 4.1. Estimates of conventions bumps from 1964 to 1980 are taken from Campbell et al. (1992, 295). Unfortunately, polling data are not abundant enough for the years prior to 1984 to graph the ebb and flow of public opinion over the course of each of these campaigns as was done for 1984 to 1992 in Figure 4.1.

6. Campbell et al. (1992) also suggest that Democratic conventions have smaller bumps than Republican conventions. However, when a dummy variable was added to this model to control for party, there was no apparent difference between Democratic and Republican bumps, all else held equal.

The Effect of Debates

O ther than the nominating conventions, presidential and vice presidential debates are easily the most visible regularly scheduled events of the campaign season. Televised debates began with a series of debates during the 1960 campaign, went on an extended hiatus during the 1964, 1968, and 1972 elections, and returned to become regular events since the 1976 election. Today, debates have become a common part of the political landscape during election years. One question concerning debates that has received mixed responses from the academic community is the degree to which debates are important political events in the campaign. Although debates are highly visible events, it is not clear that they are very important to the voting public. In this chapter, the influence of debates on the voting behavior and attitude formation of the mass public is examined.

Debates and Information

Debates serve important information functions for both candidates and voters. The candidates are given an opportunity to make their case to a vast audience of viewers, and voters are provided with information that may help to shape or reinforce opinions about the candidates. According to Diana

Table 5.1   Television Exposure of Presidential Debates, 1960-1992

Year	Percentage of Television Households	Millions of People
1960	59.9	—
1976	51.2	65.4
1980	58.9	80.6
1984	45.7	66.2
1988	36.4	66.2
1992	43.3	66.4

SOURCE: Stanley and Niemi (1994, 76).
NOTE: Entries represent the average for all presidential debates in each of the election years.

Owen (1991), the format of contemporary debates facilitates the ability of voters to gather important information about the candidates, which increases the potential effect of debates on public opinion. Because both candidates are present for a direct comparison in a single format, the viewer "can view the candidates one-on-one and contrast their viewpoints and personal styles" (Owen 1991, 111). This format, which leads Lanoue and Schrott (1991) to refer to presidential debates as "joint press conferences," does indeed provide voters with the only opportunity during the campaign to scrutinize the candidates at the same time on the same stage under identical conditions.

Perhaps just as important as the format is the magnitude of the audience reached by the debates. This audience is reached in two different ways. First, millions of people are directly exposed to the content of the debates by tuning in to watch them. Table 5.1 presents the viewing audiences for all broadcast presidential debates since the first Nixon-Kennedy debate in 1960. Although the audience share of debates has diminished over time, they still manage to reach millions of potential voters. In 1992, for instance, the three presidential debates were viewed by an average of over 66 million people. This represents a huge opportunity for candidates to convey their messages to the voting public. Second, debates project information beyond the confines of the television screen on the night of the debate. Another important avenue of influence for the debates is media coverage of the debate. In the days following the debate, the media report on what were seen as the important points in the debate and which candidate appeared to have "won" the debate. These reports may color voters' evaluations of the debates and give momentum to the declared winner (Lanoue and Schrott 1991; Lemert et al. 1991).

The most important function of debates is the provision of information. Jamieson and Birdsell (1988) point to a number of different aspects of the candidates about which debate viewers can learn: policy differences, the substance of the prospective presidencies, differences between the parties, character insights, and potential strengths and weaknesses of the prospective presidencies. Clearly, the debates have potential to provide information on many different dimensions of the candidates, information that may prove useful to voters.

Although much information is available, it will not be used in the same manner by all viewers. Different viewers have different information needs and will use the information accordingly. Kraus and Davis (1981) describe three broad groups for whom debates serve different functions. Some voters are moderately interested in the campaign and have their interest sparked by campaign events. For these individuals, the debates serve the function of providing a stimulus to become involved in the process and to learn about the candidates; what they learn from the debates may be very useful to them throughout the rest of the campaign. Another group of individuals are those who can be described as seekers of political information. These individuals already possess a lot of information and use the debates to learn more about the candidates. The information generated by debates may help people in this group reach a final voting decision. Finally, there are those for whom the debates provide little more than a reinforcing function. Members of this group, usually partisans, use the debates to reinforce and validate their previously determined views of the candidates.

Having said that debates provide the campaigns with the opportunity to educate the electorate, it is not clear that the information the candidates provide can actually persuade voters. One problem for the campaigns is that, at least for a substantial portion of the audience, the candidates are in effect "preaching to the converted." As Kraus and Davis point out, a sizable portion of the viewing audience will either have decided already how to vote or will have formed opinions about the candidates prior to the debate. For these viewers, all information provided by the debates is sifted through a perceptual screen that weighs and tries to reconcile evidence from the debate with previously held beliefs about the candidates (Lanoue and Schrott 1991; Owen 1991). Evidence of this kind of effect led Owen (1991), in her study of the 1984 and 1988 debates, to conclude that "at best, the debate format provides decided voters with the opportunity to root for their candidate under game-like conditions" (1991, 139).

Other research is more optimistic about the effect of debates on public opinion, especially candidate preferences. Of particular interest is Geer's (1988) study of the first debate of 1976 and both debates in 1984, which exercised statistical controls for preexisting attitudes toward the candidates. Geer found that debates do have the capacity to persuade voters, especially those who are cross-pressured or who have weak commitments to the candidates. Lanoue analyzed the effect of the 1980 debate (1992) and the second debate of 1988 (1991) and similarly concluded that there is evidence of a persuasive influence from debates, although this influence diminishes over time. Although the work of Geer (1988) and Lanoue (1991, 1992) focused on the effect of debates on individual voters, Shelley and Hwang, in their study of aggregate trends in the 1988 election (1991), found that the second debate of 1988 had a significant positive effect on George Bush's standing in the polls.

Some academic research, then, suggests that debates may serve as more than just opportunities for voters to root for their candidates. Debates may also play an important persuasive function. Having demonstrated quite substantial convention effects in Chapter 4, however, it is interesting to speculate about how debates differ from conventions and how this might produce different effects on public opinion. The first important difference between conventions and debates lies in the format. The candidate does not have to share the stage with the other side during a convention, whereas sharing the stage is the essence of the debate process. The very thing that Owen (1991) speculated might make debates important sources of information—allowing the viewers to make one-on-one comparisons—may actually blunt the potential effect of the event. During the convention period each side has an opportunity to make uncontested presentations to the American people. In the debate process, however, all presentations are contested—candidates are able to respond immediately to statements and accusations made by the other side. The level of contestation is heightened because presidential candidates are usually not new to the debate game; they know what to expect and they come prepared to do battle. Therefore, it is unlikely that one side's argument will be able to dominate the broadcast in any way resembling the manner that campaign messages are able to dominate during the conventions.

Another important difference between debates and conventions has to do with timing. Conventions occur during the summer when many voters have yet to make up their minds and campaign information is relatively scarce. Debates, on the other hand, occur in the fall, usually in October, when most people have made up their minds and information is less scarce and, therefore, less valuable. By this point in the campaign most of what will be said in the debates has already been conveyed in some form to the public through the campaign process and it is less likely that the electorate will learn something new during the debates. For these reasons, the pool of inducible voters is smaller during the debates than during the convention period.

All of this is not to say that debates should not be expected to have an effect on public opinion. Indeed, debates do provide massive, relatively concentrated doses of information to the electorate. Due to the format and the timing of the debates, however, one should not expect the seismic effects that are sometimes registered by conventions. Although there are many different aspects of debates that warrant empirical scrutiny, this chapter focuses on only one facet: the ability of debates to persuade voters. Specifically, the remainder of this chapter examines the persuasive effect of debates in the 1984, 1988, and 1992 elections, at both the aggregate and individual levels.

Contemporary Debates

From 1984 to 1992, presidential candidates met in seven different debates and vice presidential candidates met in three different debates. Although the debates all shared the same "press conference" format, there were many differences between them, due to the candidates, the context of the election, and some variations in the format. Many of the debates produced memorable moments, some of which were viewed by political observers as critical to the election. Also, as illustrated in Table 5.2, the public was, in most cases, able to deliver a clear verdict concerning the performance of the candidates in the debates.

THE 1984 DEBATES

In 1984 there were two presidential and debates one vice presidential debate. The first presidential debate was held in early October, when Reagan was far ahead in the polls. For the Mondale camp this was seen as a real opportunity to make headway against a very successful Reagan campaign (Germond and Witcover 1985, 293). The debate did not disappoint them. By most accounts, Mondale got the best of Reagan in their first debate. Mondale

Table 5.2   Public Assessments of Which Candidate Did the Best Job in the Debates (Who Won?)

	Democrat (%)	Republican (%)	Neither/Tie (%)	Independent (%)
1984				
First debate	61	26	13	—
Second debate	33	45	22	—
Vice presidential debate	34	48	18	—
1988				
First debate	41	43	17	—
Second debate	28	51	21	—
Vice presidential debate	55	29	16	—
1992				
First debate	36	19	9	39
Second debate	54	25	—	20
Third debate	36	21	—	26
Vice presidential debate	50	32	—	7

NOTE: All percentages from the first debate in 1984 to the first debate in 1992 are derived from the network surveys described in Appendix B. The remaining percentages for the 1992 debates were taken from postdebate network surveys as reported in *Facts on File*, which did not report the percentage who thought the debate was a tie.

did not succeed, however, by convincing viewers that he was right on the issues and Reagan was wrong; he succeeded by contrasting, with Reagan's help, his relative youth and vigor against Reagan's age and apparent inability to effectively respond to questions from the panel. The contrast was so stark that the media was consumed in the days following the debate with the issue of whether the president was too old to govern (Germond and Witcover 1985, 2). The public verdict on the debate was clear: Mondale was overwhelmingly viewed as having "won" the first debate (for all references to debate performance evaluations, see Table 5.2). After a relatively calm campaign period, the Reagan camp saw at least a potential threat to their seemingly inevitable victory.

More than anything, the first debate significantly raised the stakes for the second presidential debate and the vice presidential debate. The vice presidential debate was potentially significant for a number of reasons: First, it marked the first time a woman had taken part in the event and second, the issues raised by the first debate concerning Reagan's advanced years elevated the importance of vice presidential candidates. The debate between Bush and Ferraro was sometimes spirited, but it produced no knockout punches for either side. In the end, the public verdict was that Bush had done a better job. The second presidential debate presented the Reagan camp with an opportunity to repair the damage done by the first debate, which is exactly what they did. The highlight of this debate occurred when Reagan was asked about his age and whether age should be a consideration for voters; he turned the question around by making a joke about not holding Mondale's youth and inexperience against him. Indeed, the public verdict was that Reagan had outperformed Mondale and the Reagan image seemed to regain some of its luster.

THE 1988 DEBATES

The 1988 campaign also featured two presidential debates and one vice presidential debate. The presidential candidates first met in late September, by which point Bush had put together and maintained a fairly substantial lead over Dukakis. This debate, then, offered Dukakis a chance to gain ground on Bush, but also offered Bush a chance to shore up his support and perhaps even make more headway in the polls. The candidates focused on different themes during the debate: Dukakis focused on policy matters whereas Bush used the debate as an opportunity to paint Dukakis as being out of the mainstream (Hershey 1989, 90-91). For all practical purposes, the public verdict was that the debate was a draw. As the trailing candidate, debating to a draw was seen as a benefit for the Dukakis campaign.

Perhaps the most memorable moment of the debates, or even the entire 1988 campaign, came from the vice presidential debate. Expectations going into the debate were very clear. Dan Quayle had been severely damaged by the postconvention hoopla concerning his National Guard service, his academic record, and his ability in general. Lloyd Bentsen, on the other hand, had attained a sort of senior statesman status and was viewed by many as the stronger half of the Democratic ticket. The debaters lived up (or down) to their expectations. One issue that came up in the debate was Quayle's qualifications for the office. At one point, in response to one such question, Quayle pointed out that he had as much legislative experience as John F. Kennedy had prior to becoming president. Bentsen, in a tone bordering on outrage, responded: "Senator, I served with Jack Kennedy. I knew Jack Kennedy. Jack Kennedy was a friend of mine. Senator, you're no Jack Kennedy." This response was the sound bite of choice in the days following the debate and it will no doubt be remembered for years to come. The public verdict on the vice presidential debate was clear: By almost a 2-to-1 margin, the public thought Bentsen had bested Quayle.

The second presidential debate represented the last real chance Dukakis had to reach out to the voters and offer himself as a viable alternative to Bush. Unfortunately for Dukakis, the debate got off to a rocky and, in the eyes of some, disastrous start. Bernard Shaw, the first panelist to ask a question, asked Dukakis if he would favor the death penalty if his wife Kitty were raped and murdered. Dukakis, who had a reputation for being a cold, humorless technocrat, responded in a somewhat indifferent and unfeeling manner and recapitulated the reasons why he opposed the death penalty. In the eyes of many, Dukakis's response to this question helped to seal his fate (Germond and Witcover 1989, 16). The public response to the debate was unequivocal: A substantial plurality, and a bare majority, felt that Bush had outperformed Dukakis.

THE 1992 DEBATES

The 1992 debates were unique compared to those in 1984 and 1988. First, the debates themselves became an important issue in the campaign. The Bush campaign refused to agree to a series of debates that had been planned by a nonpartisan debate commission and several debates had to be canceled. The Clinton campaign lost no time in making political hay out Bush's refusal to debate. Much to Bush's chagrin, he was greeted at many of his campaign rallies by a Clinton supporter dressed in a chicken costume, holding a sign that referred to him as "Chicken George" because he would not commit to a debating schedule. The conclusion of the debate over debates began when Bush challenged Clinton to a series of four presidential and two vice presidential debates. The two camps finally decided on three presidential debates and one vice presidential debate, to be held over a period of eight days in mid-October. These debates were also unique because the format varied from one debate to the next and, more important, they involved the participation of independent candidate Ross Perot.

There were no knockout punches landed in any of the presidential debates. At times, however, it seemed that instead of three candidates debating each other there were two, Clinton and Perot, debating one, President Bush. The Perot strategy, especially in the first two debates, appeared to be to hold his fire on Clinton and use most of his ammunition on Bush. On balance, having to debate two opponents seems to have hurt Bush's performance; he was not seen as having won any of the debates. The first debate was a virtual toss-up between Clinton and Perot; Clinton won the second debate quite handily; and Clinton edged out Perot in the third debate.

The vice presidential debate was a lively affair, featuring Dan Quayle in an attack mode, Albert Gore in a mostly defensive posture, and James Stockdale, Perot's running mate, appearing out of his element. To a large extent, Quayle set the tone of the debate with persistent attacks on Clinton's record and on his character. The attack mode did not win many points in the eyes of the public, however, as the postdebate polls showed that the public viewed Gore as the winner of the debate.

The Aggregate Effect of Debates

The debates from 1984 to 1992 took place in a number of different circumstances and produced a number of different outcomes. Immediately following any debate the question on participants' minds is how the debate will play with the public. In particular, the campaigns are concerned with which candidate the public will view as having "won" the debate. As the preceding discussion and Table 5.2 illustrate, sometimes the public sees a clear winner and other times it is not clear that one candidate delivered a stronger performance than the other. Ultimately, though, the question of who won the debate is important only because it may help one candidate gain an advantage over the other. All candidates hope that their performance, or more precisely the public's perception of their performance, will translate into a gain in their standing in the polls.

Figure 5.1 and Table 5.3 shed some light on the aggregate effect of presidential and vice presidential debates on candidate support during the campaign. In Figure 5.1, the percentage point Republican advantage or deficit (negative numbers) over the Democratic candidate is plotted over a period spanning one week before the first debate to one week after the last debate. From this figure it is apparent that there is significant movement in public opinion following presidential debates, although the amount of movement varies from debate to debate and from year to year. The biggest swings in opinion appear to be associated with both presidential debates in 1984 and the last presidential debates of 1988 and 1992. In many cases, however, what

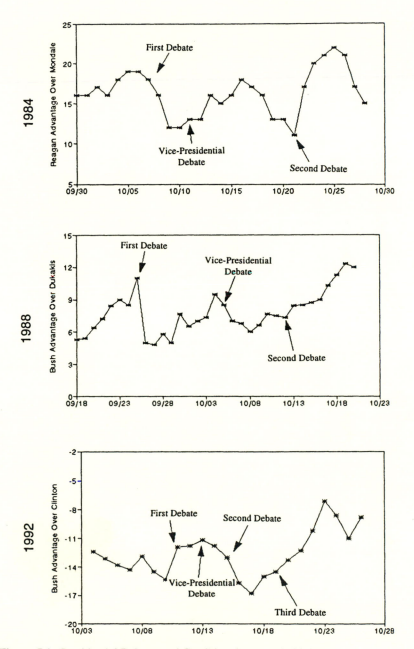

Figure 5.1. Presidential Debates and Candidate Support, 1984-1992

Table 5.3   The Impact of Presidential Debates on Candidate Support, 1984-1992

	Predebate Vote	*Postdebate Vote*	*Debate Bump*
1984 debates			
First presidential	+17.3R	+13.8R	+3.5D
Second presidential	+15.5R	+18.9R	+3.4R
Vice presidential	+16.3R	+15.9R	+0.4D
1988 debates			
First presidential	+6.8R	+6.0R	+0.8D
Second presidential	+7.0R	+9.8R	+2.8R
Vice presidential	+7.0R	+7.0R	0
1992 debates			
First presidential	+13.8D	+13.6D	+0.2R
Second presidential	+12.8D	+13.9D	+1.1D
Third presidential	+13.6D	+10.2D	+3.4R
Vice presidential	+13.1D	+14.3D	+1.2D

NOTE: All entries in the first two columns are the percentage-point advantage held by the leading candidate (D = Democrat, R = Republican). These percentages are based on an average of polls taken during the week before and the week following the day of the debate. The third column represents the amount and direction of change in candidate support following the debates.

seems to be a shift in opinion immediately following the debate appears to recede back toward the predebate level of support within a few days.

Table 5.3 summarizes the patterns in Figure 5.1 in terms of percentage point gains or losses for the candidates. Here, the average level of candidate support over the seven days prior to the debate is compared to the level of support over the seven days following the debate. Comparing support over a span of two weeks should be enough to capture not only whatever "bump" that might occur following the debate but should also take into account the degree to which the bump dissipates after just a few days.

Several important findings present themselves in Table 5.3. First, presidential debates can produce significant changes in candidate support. In each of the three years, at least one of the debates generated shifts of nearly 3 to 3.5 points in the polls. In 1984, Mondale made significant gains in the first debate, only to be almost completely offset by Reagan's performance in the second debate. In the second debate of 1988, Bush's perceived performance was strong enough to increase his standing by almost 3 percentage points. In 1992, Bush gained significant ground on Clinton following the third debate. Second, although presidential debates do sometimes produce significant changes in candidate support, this is not always the case. For instance, there was very little change in candidate standing following the first debate of 1988 and the first two debates of 1992. For all practical purposes, these debates barely produced a ripple in public opinion. Finally, there is very little evidence that vice presidential debates do much at all to alter the political landscape; none of the three vice presidential debates examined here produce a substantial aggregate effect.[1] Even in 1988, when Bentsen appeared to draw blood with his comment that Quayle was "no Jack Kennedy," there was no movement in the polls. The public response following this and other vice presidential debates can be described as weak at best.

Comparing the debate bumps in Table 5.3 with the trends in public perceptions of debate performance in Table 5.2, it is clear that there is a tendency for the apparently victorious debater to experience some degree of surge in public support following the debate. In 1984, Mondale was seen as winning the first debate and he experienced a bump of about 3.5 percentage points; Reagan was seen as having won the second debate and won back nearly all of the support that had drifted to Mondale. In 1988, there was no clear winner of the first debate and only a very slight movement in the polls following the debate; however, when Bush was seen as the clear winner of the second debate he gained almost three points in the polls. In 1992, the first debate was a toss-up between Clinton and Perot and there was virtually no change in the balance of support between Bush and Clinton; in the second debate, Clinton was the clear winner and saw a slight bump in the polls. The third debate of 1992 does not fit the pattern of the other debates. George Bush was clearly judged to have come in third in the debate, with Clinton coming in second, but Bush gained more than 3 percentage points on Clinton following the debate.

The close relationship between debate verdict and postdebate opinion bump is depicted in Figure 5.2, in which the independent variable (horizontal axis) is the net performance rating of the Republican candidate (percentage of respondents saying the Republican won minus the percentage who said the Democrat won) and the dependent variable is the change in the Republican candidate's relative standing in the polls (based on Table 5.3). Clearly, there is a strong linear relationship between a candidate's debate performance evaluation and size of the postdebate bump. Generally speaking, when candidates are judged to have done better in a debate than their opponent, they can expect to see some increase in support in the postdebate period. The one case that is somewhat distinct from the others is the third debate in 1992,

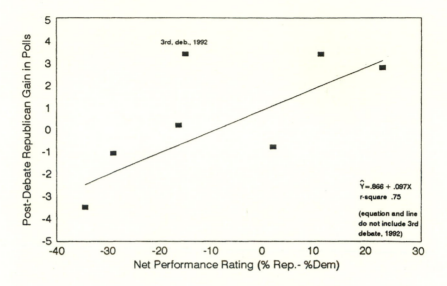

Figure 5.2. Debate Performance and Postdebate Bumps, 1984-1992

in which Bush was judged to have done considerably worse than Clinton but still saw an increase in his poll numbers. Setting this observation aside (it will be dealt with in the next section), a regression analysis of the remaining debates (see regression line and equation in Figure 5.2) suggests that, starting with a base of .87 percentage points, for every percentage point advantage (disadvantage) in the public's assessment of who won a particular debate, a candidate should receive a gain (loss) of .097 points in his relative poll standing. According to this regression analysis, debate performance evaluations explain 75% of the variation in postdebate poll bumps.[2]

Although this result indicates a clear linear relationship, it also points to the limited effect debates can have on public opinion. Consider, for example, a hypothetical case in which 20% of the population considered Candidate A to have won the debate, 70% thought Candidate B won, and 10% thought it was a tie. In this case, Candidate B holds a 50 percentage point advantage in the postdebate public verdict over Candidate A. According to the analysis in Figure 5.2, this huge disparity in perceived performances, which is far greater than anything in Table 5.2, can be expected to increase Candidate B's standing by about 5.7 percentage points, a bump that is not inconsequential but that is hardly of the magnitude found with postconvention bumps. In fact, in the elections analyzed here, a bump of this magnitude during the debate period would have made little difference in most cases. Only in 1988 would a bump of this magnitude, in Dukakis's favor, really have changed the nature of the race—even then it would only have made the race more competitive.

A CLOSER LOOK AT 1992

The third debate in 1992 stands out as an outlier in Figure 5.2. Following that debate, George Bush gained 3.4 points on his Democratic rival, Bill Clinton, even though the public saw Clinton as having given a stronger performance than Bush. The most obvious explanation for this bizarre finding lies in one of the unique features of the 1992 election: the presence of a strong independent candidate, Ross Perot. Perot was being taken seriously as an alternative candidate and had finished a strong second in public evaluations of the candidates' performances in the third debate. One possible explanation for the peculiar consequences of the third debate is that Perot benefited from a strong second-place showing in the last debate and took more support from Clinton than he did from Bush as his poll numbers increased. Given that Clinton and Perot were sharing the anti-Bush vote, either candidate's increase in the polls would probably be achieved at the expense of the other.

Evidence supporting this trade-off is presented in Figure 5.3, which plots the candidates' standing in the polls during the debate period (one week before the first debate to one week after the last debate). The left vertical axis represents the Bush and Clinton trial-heat results and the right vertical axis represents Perot's trial-heat results. Overlaying Perot's standing against the other two candidates' makes it possible to see the degree to which there is a trade-off in support among the candidates. The strongest trend throughout the debate period is a decline in support for Clinton and a concomitant increase in support for Perot. Compared to the Clinton and Perot patterns, Bush's support was relatively constant during this time period. There was a slight decline in Bush support following the second debate but this appears to have been just a temporary shift. This trend appears to represent a clear trade-off between Clinton and Perot support. This trade-off is supported by an analysis of the correlation between the levels of candidate support after Perot entered the race. From October 1 to November 1, the correlation between Bush support and Perot support was –.24 (not significant), whereas

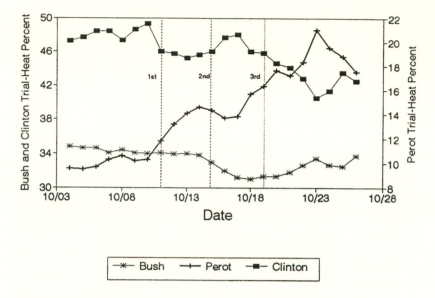

Figure 5.3. Poll Standings of the Three Candidates During the 1992 Debates

the correlation between Clinton support and Perot support was –.81, indicating that whenever Clinton or Perot gained support, it was primarily at the expense of the other.

Table 5.4 summarizes the gains and losses incurred by each of the candidates during the 1992 debate period. These data confirm that any gain Bush made on Clinton during the debates was the result of Clinton losing support rather than Bush gaining support. Following each of the three debates, Bush actually lost some degree of popular support; he managed only to gain ground on Clinton following the third debate because Clinton lost even more support than Bush as people moved over to the Perot campaign.

Perot was in fact the main beneficiary of the 1992 debates. Although he "won" only the first debate, finished last in the second debate, and came in a strong second in the last debate, Perot gained supporters following each debate. The most plausible reason for Perot's strong showing is that, to the degree that people really "needed" any information about the candidates at this late stage of the campaign, they needed information about Perot. Perot had officially been in the race for only ten days before the first debate and had not had the luxury of holding an attention-grabbing convention. In fact, although Perot had been a very visible figure during the spring and early

Table 5.4   A Closer Look at the 1992 Presidential Debates

	Predebate Support (%)	Postdebate Support (%)	Debate Bump
First debate			
Bush	34.4	32.7	−1.7
Clinton	48.1	46.3	−1.8
Perot	10.0	14.2	+4.2
Second debate			
Bush	34.0	31.6	−2.4
Clinton	46.8	45.6	−1.2
Perot	12.1	17.1	+5.0
Third debate			
Bush	32.7	32.6	−0.1
Clinton	46.3	42.8	−3.5
Perot	14.2	18.6	+4.4

NOTE: The candidate support statistic is the percentage of all decided respondents who intend to vote for the candidate. The percentages are based on an average of polls taken between seven days before and seven days after the debate.

summer, people had a lot to learn about him. In effect, the debates served as Perot's convention; they gave him an opportunity to present himself to the American people in a very visible format at a time when people had limited information about him. Judging from his ascent in the polls, some people liked what they saw.

Of course, it must be remembered that this was also the period during which Perot was launching a media blitz that included not only campaign ads but also thirty-minute chunks of airtime that Perot used to air what might be called "infomercials" about his candidacy. During these extended campaign commercials, Perot sat at a desk and delivered lectures, with the aid of some simple charts and graphs, about the problems facing the country. Voters were being exposed to many other sources of information about Perot during this time period, which apparently contributed to an increase in his poll standing—an increase that hurt the Clinton campaign and made the contest between Bush and Clinton more competitive.

AGGREGATE EFFECTS

Debates have the potential to help or hurt the political fortunes of the participating candidates. Over the period examined here there was a generally predictable effect from presidential debates: The political consequence of a debate is positively related to the degree to which the public felt the candidates had performed well in the debate. Generally speaking, the "winning" debater stands to make a modest gain in the polls. The exception to this pattern is the 1992 debates—in particular, the third debate—in which independent candidate Ross Perot gained support throughout the debate period regardless of his perceived debate performance. Perot's climb in the polls generally occurred at Clinton's expense regardless of how Clinton performed in the debates, which resulted in a narrowing of the race between Clinton and Bush.

There is little evidence here that vice presidential debates have any consistent effect on candidate standing. Even in the wake of very lopsided outcomes, such as the 1988 debate between Dan Quayle and Lloyd Bentsen, there appears to be little consequence for the presidential race.

Individual-Level Evidence

The preceding analysis focused on the aggregate effect of presidential debates on public opinion during the campaign. In some cases the debates had a clear effect, providing the winning candidate with a boost in support. In other cases the effect of the debate was less decisive. The reason debates manifest themselves as changes in candidate support is assumed to be because they have an effect on the way individuals feel about the candidates. In this section, the analysis shifts from aggregate outcomes to the effect of debates on the individual voters—in particular, the effect of debates on individual vote choice and candidate evaluations.

VOTE CHOICE

The ultimate objective of candidates in a debate is to persuade voters either to vote for them or to vote against the other candidate. One difficulty encountered when studying whether candidates are able to persuade voters during the debates, however, is that the perceptions of most viewers are colored by their political predispositions going into the debate (Geer 1988; Lanoue and Schrott 1991; Owen 1991). The single best predictor of which candidate a viewer thought won a given debate is that viewer's predebate vote choice; most people think their candidate won. Therefore, when one finds a strong correlation between debate evaluation (who "won") and postdebate vote intention, it does not necessarily represent the influence of the debate on vote choice. Instead, both debate evaluation and postdebate vote intention may reflect the influence of predebate vote choice. In addition to predebate vote choice, myriad other variables—such as partisanship, ideology, presidential approval, and candidate assessments—are likely to influence debate evaluations and postdebate vote choice.

To appropriately analyze the effect of debate evaluations on vote choice at the individual level, then, it is necessary to impose strict controls for predebate political predispositions. The best way to accomplish this is to use a panel survey in which respondents are interviewed both before and after the debate. Questions from the predebate survey can then be used to measure predebate political predispositions and questions in the postdebate interview can be used to measure the debate evaluation and postdebate political attitudes. Fortunately, just such data are available for many of the debates that were analyzed in the preceding section. For all debates in 1984 and 1988 and the first debate of 1992, *CBS News* and the *New York Times* conducted panel surveys that included predebate and postdebate interviews, thus allowing for the appropriate control of predebate attitudes. These surveys are used in the following analyses and are described in greater detail in Appendix B.

Table 5.5 lists and defines a group of variables that are used to analyze the effect of debate performance evaluations on vote choice. The dependent variable in this analysis is the respondent's postdebate vote intention. The independent variables include a number of controls for predebate political predispositions: predebate vote choice, party identification, political ideology, net candidate assessment, and presidential approval. Again, these variables are included to control for preexisting nondebate factors that could influence both debate evaluation and postdebate vote choice. The remaining independent variable is debate evaluation, which was ascertained following the debate.[3] The presence of several predebate predisposition variables in the model provides a rigorous test of the effect of debate evaluations on vote choice. A significant effect from the debate evaluation variable in such a model reflects the effect of debate evaluations after taking into account the influence of predebate vote choice and a number of other measures of predebate political predispositions.

The logistic regression analysis of the effect of debate evaluations, controlling for political predispositions, is presented in Table 5.6. In this table the coefficients represent the effect of the independent variables on the

Table 5.5   Description of Variables Used in Vote Choice Model

---

Dependent variable
Postdebate vote choice
(0 = Democrat, 1 = Republican)

Predebate independent variables
Predebate vote choice
(0 = Democrat, 1 = Republican)

Party identification
(1 = Democrat, 2 = Independent leaning Democrat, 3 = Independent, 4 = Independent
leaning Republican, 5 = Republican)

Ideology
(1 = Liberal, 2 = Moderate, 3 = Conservative)

Candidate assessment
The difference between the overall assessment of the Republican candidate
(1 = Unfavorable, 2 = Undecided/not heard enough, 3 = Favorable) and the assessment of
the Democratic candidate (range −2 to +2)

Presidential approval
(1 = Approve of the job the president is doing, 0 = Disapprove)

Postdebate variable
Debate performance evaluation
Opinion on which candidate did the best job during the debate (−1 = Democrat won,
0 = tie, 1 = Republican won)

---

likelihood of voting Republican in the postdebate period. As expected, predebate political predispositions are strongly related to postdebate vote choice; this is especially true for predebate vote choice, candidate assessment, and to a lesser degree, presidential approval.[4] No doubt, the effect of these variables, especially predebate vote choice, go a long way toward accounting for the strong explanatory power of the model.

Most important, debate performance evaluations demonstrate a significant effect on postdebate vote choice in each of the periods in Table 5.6, even in the presence of strong controls for predebate attitudes. These coefficients should be interpreted as meaning that, regardless of predebate attitudes, thinking that one candidate won the debate makes respondents more likely to support that candidate than they would have been had they thought the other candidate won or that the debate was a tie. This is not the same as saying that thinking a candidate won the debate leads one to vote for that candidate,

Table 5.6   Logistic Regression Analysis of the Impact of Debate Performance Evaluations on Postdebate Vote Intention, Controlling for Predebate Political Predispositions

	1984		1988		1992
	1st Debate	2nd Debate	1st Debate	2nd Debate	1st Debate
Constant	−3.68**	−2.73**	−2.32	−2.26	−2.54**
	(0.86)	(1.21)	(1.62)	(1.53)	(1.20)
Predebate variables					
Vote intention	4.06**	2.91**	3.96**	2.64**	2.64**
	(0.71)	(.71)	(1.07)	(.92)	(.95)
Candidate assessment	.71**	1.86**	.63	1.65**	1.16**
	(0.22)	(.41)	(.43)	(.46)	(.40)
Party identification	.59**	.46	.01	.05	−.15
	(0.14)	(.34)	(.24)	(.21)	(.25)
Ideology	.42	.16	.32	.26	.39
	(0.33)	(.36)	(.57)	(.51)	(.48)
Presidential approval	—	−.65	.27	1.48**	1.24*
	—	(.90)	(.83)	(.74)	(.69)
Postdebate attitudes					
Debate performance	1.87**	1.57**	1.81**	3.12**	1.83**
	(.39)	(.40)	(.45)	(.65)	(.46)
Percentage correct	95.8	97.2	96.9	94.7	94.1
PRE	0.89	0.93	0.93	0.87	0.82
Chi-square	736.6	677.7	335	374.9	258.2
N	709	570	291	322	269

*p < .10; **p < .05.

only that making such evaluations increases the likelihood of voting for that candidate.

Although debate evaluations significantly affect candidate preference, their effect is constrained by the influence of predebate predispositions. This constraint is demonstrated in Table 5.7, which summarizes the effect of debate evaluations on the probability of voting Republican, controlling for predebate vote choice. The entries in this table represent the probability of a respondent expressing a postdebate Republican vote intention under different combinations of debate evaluations and predebate vote choice. In calculating these probabilities it was assumed that the respondent was average on

Table 5.7 The Impact of Debate Performance Assessments on the Probability of Voting Republican, Controlling for Predebate Vote Intention

1984

Debate Winner	Predebate (1st) Vote		Predebate (2nd) Vote	
	Mondale	Reagan	Mondale	Reagan
Mondale	0.07	0.81	0.07	0.59
Neither	0.32	0.97	0.27	0.87
Reagan	0.75	0.99	0.65	0.97
Potential impact	0.68	0.18	0.58	0.38

1988

Debate Winner	Predebate (1st) Vote		Predebate (2nd) Vote	
	Dukakis	Bush	Dukakis	Bush
Dukakis	0.04	0.70	0.03	0.28
Neither	0.20	0.93	0.39	0.90
Bush	0.63	0.99	0.93	0.99
Potential impact	0.59	0.29	0.90	0.71

1992

Debate Winner	Predebate (1st) Vote	
	Clinton/Perot	Bush
Clinton/Perot	0.02	0.23
Neither	0.12	0.65
Bush	0.46	0.93
Potential impact	0.44	0.70

NOTE: All cell entries reflect the probability of voting Republican. The probabilities are based on the logistic regression analysis presented in Table 5.6. The potential impact is a measure of the difference in the probability of voting Republican associated with different debate performance assessments, and is calculated by subtracting the lowest probability value in each column from the highest value in each column.

all other independent variables. Several interesting findings are apparent in this table. First, the potential effect of the debate on individual voters varies substantially from debate to debate. The smallest potential effect occurred among Reagan supporters in the first debate of 1984. Reagan supporters who thought Mondale had won the first debate were only slightly less likely to continue supporting Reagan than those who thought Reagan had won the debate. The greatest potential effect occurred among Dukakis supporters in the second debate of 1988; Dukakis supporters who thought Dukakis had won the debate were almost certain to continue supporting Dukakis, and those who thought Bush had won the debate were almost certain to change their candidate preference.

Second, debate evaluations also have the potential to change vote intention in many other cases. Of course, this finding must be tempered with the knowledge that there is a very strong tendency for people to think their preferred candidate won the debate. There is also a tendency for supporters of the trailing candidate to be more easily swayed than those who support the leading candidate. This is the case in each of the debates examined in Table 5.7. Third, although debate evaluations clearly have an effect on vote intention, predebate vote choice appears to have a much more dramatic effect. In twenty-four of the thirty entries in Table 5.7 respondents continued to support their predebate candidate regardless of debate evaluations. In only six entries were respondents likely to change their candidate preference in response to their debate performance evaluation. Debate evaluations, then, can influence the probability of supporting a candidate, but the debate performance evaluation is not nearly as important a determinant of postdebate candidate preference as is predebate candidate preference. Still, the significant effect of debates does indicate that they are a notable source of influence on individual voting behavior.

CANDIDATE EVALUATIONS

In addition to influencing voting behavior, presidential debates may also influence the perceptions voters have about personal characteristics of the candidates. In fact, it is expected that part of the reason debates have an influence on voting behavior is that they change the way people perceive the candidates. Once again, however, it is necessary to exercise caution when examining the relationship between debate performance evaluations and candidate assessments. As was the case with vote choice, it is likely that predebate political predispositions will color postdebate candidate evaluations. Therefore, it is once again necessary to control for political predispositions when examining the relationship between debate performance evaluations and postdebate candidate evaluations.

The research strategy used to measure the effect of debate evaluations on candidate assessments is the same as was used in the voting model: The model includes a set of variables to control for predebate attitudes, one of which is the predebate candidate evaluation. By lagging the dependent variable and controlling for the effects of other predebate attitudes, the effect of debate evaluations should be purged of any contamination from political predispositions.

Unfortunately, not all of the surveys used in the vote analysis included questions about candidate characteristics in both the pre- and postdebate surveys. There were, however, enough usable items to analyze the effect of debates on candidate evaluations for the first presidential debate in 1984 and both debates in 1988. The measures of candidate evaluations to be examined here are presented in Table 5.8 and represent respondent perceptions of (1) the degree to which the candidates care about people, (2) the degree to which the candidates demonstrate leadership qualities, (3) the degree to which the respondent agrees with the candidates on issues, (4) how well the candidates understand the problems a president has to deal with, and (5) net candidate assessment. The third dependent variable listed is less a measure of a candidate's personal characteristics than the others; instead, it is a measure of how close the respondent feels to the candidates on the issue of the day. This variable is included in the analysis because it, like the other variables, represents a comparative evaluation of the candidates, albeit in a slightly different manner than the other dependent variables.

The analysis of these measures of candidate evaluation is presented in Table 5.9 where, once again, there is a pattern of relationships very similar to those found in the vote choice analysis. First, predebate attitudes, especially the predebate candidate evaluations, are strongly related to postdebate candidate evaluations. This confirms that predebate predispositions color postdebate attitudes. Second, there is strong support for the hypothesis that debates influence public opinion. Even in the presence of lagged dependent variables and other control variables for predebate political predispositions, debate performance evaluations exerted significant influence on candidate evaluations in four of the five equations. The only time the debate did not

Table 5.8   Description of Dependent Variables Used in the Candidate Evaluation
Model

Care about people
  Based on questions that asked if the respondent thought the candidates cared about people
  (–1 = Mondale/not Reagan, 0 = neither/both, +1 = Reagan/not Mondale)

Leadership
  Based on questions that asked if the respondent thought the candidates were strong leaders
  (–1 = Mondale/not Reagan, 0 = neither/both, +1 = Reagan/not Mondale)

Agree
  Based on a question that asked respondents, regardless of who they intended to vote for,
  which candidate's positions they agreed with more (–1 = Dukakis, 0 = neither/both, +1 = Bush)

Understand
  Based on questions that asked if the respondents thought the candidates understood the
  complicated problems a president has to deal with (–1 = Dukakis/not Bush, 0 = neither/both,
  +1 = Bush/not Dukakis)

Candidate assessment
  The difference between the overall assessment of the Republican candidate
  (1 = unfavorable, 2 = undecided/not heard enough, 3 = favorable) and the assessment of the
  Democratic candidate (range –2 to +2)

---

have a significant influence was when the dependent variable was the degree
to which the respondent felt the candidates cared about people. In all other
cases debate performance evaluations have a significant influence on postdebate evaluations of candidate characteristics. Specifically, the better a
respondent's evaluation of a candidate's debate performance relative to the
other candidate, the more likely that the respondent will give a more positive
evaluation of that candidate in the postdebate period than was given in the
predebate period, all else held constant. This finding holds up not just for
those dependent variables that are clearly indicators of candidate characteristics but also for the dependent variable that measures the degree to which
the respondent agrees with the candidates' issue positions.

Conclusion

The analysis presented in this chapter demonstrates that presidential
debates often play an important, persuasive role in the campaign process.

Table 5.9   The Impact of Debate Performance Evaluations on Attitudes
Toward Presidential Candidates, Controlling for Predebate Attitudes
(OLS Regression)

Dependent Variable	First Debate, 1984		First Debate, 1988		Second Debate, 1988
	Care About People	Leader	Agree	Understand	Candidate Assessment
Constant	−.10	−.03	−.03	−.13	−.63
	(.07)	(.09)	(.11)	(.12)	(.18)
Predebate variables					
Care about people	.65**	—	—	—	—
	(.05)	—	—	—	—
Leadership	—	.36**	—	—	—
	—	(.05)	—	—	—
Agree with candidate	—	—	.51**	—	—
	—	—	(.06)	—	—
Candidate understands	—	—	—	.32**	—
	—	—	—	(.06)	—
Candidate assessment	.08**	.19**	.08**	.03	.50**
	(.02)	(.03)	(.03)	(.03)	(.08)
Party identification	.03*	.05**	.05**	−.03	.07*
	(.02)	(.02)	(.02)	(.02)	(.04)
Ideology	−.03	−.001	.05	.07*	.10
	(.03)	(.04)	(.04)	(.04)	(.07)
Presidential approval	—	—	.11	.31**	.35**
	—	—	(.09)	(.08)	(.12)
Postdebate attitudes					
Debate performance	.03	.12**	.22**	.22**	.60**
Evaluation	(.03)	(.03)	(.04)	(.05)	(.08)
R^2	0.71	0.66	0.81	0.57	0.77
N	346	330	275	257	333

NOTE: Standard errors are in parentheses.
*$p < .10$; **$p < .05$.

Several pieces of evidence point in this direction. First, it has been demonstrated that debates usually produce a bump in support for the candidate who

is judged to have delivered the strongest performance. The magnitude of the postdebate bump is usually in proportion to the degree to which the public considers the candidate to have won the debate. Second, in addition to these aggregate shifts in candidate support it has been demonstrated that individuals can be persuaded to change their vote intention based on their judgment of who won the debates. Even when controlling for predebate vote choice and predispositions, it was shown that evaluations of debate performance significantly influence postdebate vote intention. Third, it has also been shown that exposure to debates influences a vast array of postdebate candidate evaluations, even in the presence of rigorous predebate control variables.

There are limits, however, to the potential effect of debates on both aggregate and individual-level outcomes. First, although there are frequently postdebate bumps in public support for the "winning" candidates, it is unlikely that the bump will be of a magnitude sufficient to alter the course of the race unless the race is extremely close going into the debate. Second, although the debates have an influence on postdebate vote intention, this effect is tempered by the fact that most respondents think their preferred candidate won the debate. Respondents who are dissatisfied with their candidate's performance are more likely to say the debate was a tie than to admit to themselves and to others that their candidate lost.

Debates, like conventions, are information-generating events. Also like conventions, debates have the potential to influence the campaign. The potential is less for debates, however, for two reasons. First, the format does not allow participants the opportunity to convey a well-crafted, uncontested message. Second, debates occur at the end of the campaign when people have already been exposed to vast amounts of campaign information and most people have already decided how they will vote. The combination of these two factors tends to blunt the effect of the messages conveyed through the debate process. The end result is that the candidates are able to use debates as a tool of persuasion, but much less successfully than they are able to use conventions for the same purpose.

Notes

1. According to Holbrook (1994) vice presidential debates more consistently produce an aggregate effect on evaluations of candidate characteristics than on aggregate vote choice. There is, however, a significant influence from vice presidential debates on individual vote choice.

2. When the third debate of 1992 is added to the analysis, the equation changes to

$$Y = 1.35 + .087X$$

where X is the net debate performance evaluation. The R^2 is smaller but is still a very substantial .49. Hence, although adding the third debate of 1992 to the analysis changes the results somewhat, the conclusion is still that the debate bump is contingent on public perceptions of debate performance.

3. With the exception of the first debate of 1992, respondents simply answered that one of the two candidates won the debate, that it was a tie, or that neither candidate won. In 1992, however, respondents sometimes answered that more than one candidate won the debate. In 1992, candidates were given credit for all responses that mentioned them as winners, even if other candidates were mentioned.

4. The presidential approval question was not asked in the survey for the first debate of 1984.

Campaigns,
National Conditions, and
U.S. Presidential Elections

The analysis and discussion in Chapters 4 and 5 demonstrated that the major events of the presidential campaign—conventions and debates—usually produce significant changes in candidate support during the campaign. But that is not the end of the story. There are, of course, other factors that influence candidate support. First, there are other factors associated with the campaign that may influence public opinion. Specifically, there are other less noticeable and presumably less consequential campaign events. Second, there is also the phenomenon of momentum, which has been found to be an important factor in primary elections. Third, candidate support is also expected to be influenced by the prevailing national political and economic climate. In this chapter, these additional sources of influence are integrated with conventions and debates into a single model that illustrates the combined effects of campaigns and national conditions on candidate support in U.S. presidential elections. This model is then tested using data from the 1984, 1988, and 1992 presidential campaigns.

Subordinate Campaign Effects

CAMPAIGN EVENTS

Although conventions and debates are clearly the major events of the presidential campaign, they are hardly the only events that generate information or have potential to influence voters. Before, during, and after these major events, there are a number of other important campaign events also taking place. Indeed, campaign events are always occurring; on any given day, the candidates and their organizations are out creating events and trying to grab the public's attention. As mentioned in Chapter 3, examples of such events are vice presidential candidate selection, major campaign speeches, major endorsements, changes in campaign strategy, campaign gaffes or scandals, and campaign staff shake-ups.

Assessing the effect of these events is important because they occur throughout the campaign and may significantly affect candidate support. Although these events may not be as important as the conventions and debates, they are still very important to an understanding of campaign dynamics. The difficulty, however, lies in quantifying these effects. First, it must be decided which events warrant attention. The number of different types of campaign "events" is virtually limitless. Every time a campaign acts, it produces an event of some kind, whether in the form of campaign advertisements, direct voter contact, rallies, local campaign activity, or some other form of activity. Because events are always occurring, it is impractical to try to include every event from the universe of campaign events. Instead, the approach taken here is to account for the influence of what appear to be the most important events during the campaign. In doing so, this analysis sets a low threshold test for the effects of campaign events: If what appear to be the most important events in a campaign do not have a significant influence on candidate support, then it is unlikely that other, less consequential events have any effect.[1]

Several criteria are used to select events for this analysis. First, the event had to be clearly related to the campaign or the activities of someone involved in the campaign. Second, the event had to be significant enough to generate exposure in the mass media. Events produce an effect because of what people learn from them. If an event receives no attention from the media, voters are unlikely to have any exposure to it and it cannot produce an effect. The third criteria is that the event had to be such that its effect could reasonably be expected to influence public opinion in favor of one candidate over the other. In other words, the direction of the effect must be clear. An example of a campaign event with an ambiguous effect occurred in 1988 when John Sasso rejoined the Dukakis campaign. Sasso was a seasoned campaign expert and might be expected to bring rigor and expertise to the Dukakis campaign. On the other hand, Sasso was a controversial figure who left the Dukakis campaign during the primary season when it was revealed that he played a role in exposing plagiarism on the part of then-rival candidate Joe Biden. Sasso's rejoining the campaign might also be viewed as a sign that the campaign was in trouble. Whether bringing Sasso on board should be expected to help or hurt Dukakis is unclear. An event such as this cannot be quantified as having a clearly anticipated directional effect.

These criteria are admittedly vague, and the process of selecting events is somewhat ad hoc in nature and invites some degree of arbitrary decision making concerning which events to analyze. When looking back at the campaigns, for instance, it is difficult not to be influenced by what seemed to be important events at the time they occurred. However, using these criteria, it is possible to cull a manageable list of events from the infinite number of campaign events that took place.

Table 6.1 presents the list of campaign events from the 1984, 1988, and 1992 campaigns that are included in this analysis. Along with the list of events and the days on which they occurred, the expected effect of the event is also indicated. Specifically, the parentheses indicate whether the event is expected to increase (+) or decrease (-) the relative poll standing of the Republican candidate. The list includes events that evolved from both the Republican and Democratic campaigns. Therefore, an event originating from the Democratic campaign that is expected to help the Democratic candidate, such as Clinton naming Gore as his running mate, should have a negative effect on the Republican position in the polls. The opposite is true for Democratic events, such as Ferraro's tax problems, that are expected to hurt the Democratic candidate and help the Republican candidate.

Having defined the list of events, the next step is to quantify the events. One alternative is to create dichotomous variables representing the effect of each event. The problem with this approach, however, is that it would be very cumbersome, requiring fifty-four separate variables, and would create severe problems with collinearity. In addition, this approach would generate event-specific explanations that do not reveal anything about the effect of events in general. To avoid these problems, a cumulative events tally variable is created that measures the changes in events over time. To create this

Table 6.1   Important Campaign Events, 1984-1992

1984	
June 6	Mondale claims nomination (–)
June 12	Mondale announces beginning of V.P. search (–)
June 14	Reagan holds press conference, announces that he is willing to meet with Soviets anytime (+)
June 21	Mondale interviews Tom Bradley for V.P. slot (–)
June 23	Mondale interviews Bentsen and Feinstein for V.P. slot (–)
June 26	Mondale and Hart meet to show unity (–)
June 28	Reagan announces plans to improve ties with USSR (+)
July 12	Mondale announces V.P. choice (–)
July 14	Mondale tries to replace Manatt with Lance (+)
July 24	Reagan holds press conference (+)
August 11	Reagan jokes about bombing USSR (–)
August 12	Potential problems with Ferraro's taxes announced (+)
August 20	Ferraro produces tax records (+)
August 21	Ferraro discusses taxes at press conference (+)
August 25	Mondale meets with Democratic governors (–)
August 28	John Anderson endorses Mondale (–)
August 29	Mondale meets with Democratic mayors (–)
September 2	Mondale launches attack on religious bigotry (–)
September 12	House Ethics Committee announces it will investigate Ferraro's finances (+)
October 4	Bush forced to pay back taxes to IRS (–)
October 8	*Wall Street Journal* and *NBC News* both question whether Reagan is too old to be effective (–)
1988	
June 8	Dukakis endorsed by Simon, Gephardt, Babbit, and Cuomo (–)
June 16	Gore endorses Dukakis (–)
July 12	Dukakis announces VP choice (–)
July 29	Dukakis denies he has suffered from clinical depression (+)
August 4	Dukakis holds rally in Philadelphia, MS without mentioning slain civil rights workers (+)
August 6	James Baker leaves administration to join Bush campaign (+)
August 16	Quayle announced as Bush's V.P. choice (+)
August 26	Bush raises pledge of allegiance and prison furlough issues (+)
September 1	Bush visits Boston Harbor (+)
September 11	Malek resigns from Bush campaign (–)
September 20	Bush visits flag factory (+)
September 22	Boston police union endorses Bush (+)
October 3	Bush's "Revolving Prison Door" ad begins (+)
October 19	Bush's "Tank" ad begins (+)
October 24	Dukakis launches talk show blitz (–)

Table 6.1   Continued

1992

June 3	Clinton appears on *Arsenio Hall Show* (–)
June 4	Bush holds news conference, most questions focus on campaign (+)
June 13	Clinton denounces Sister Souljah's lyrics (–)
June 15	Quayle "potato(e)" incident in New Jersey (–)
June 19	Quayle blasts "Cultural Elite" (+)
June 21	Clinton releases economic plan (–)
July 9	Clinton picks Gore as V.P. (–)
July 17-22	Clinton/Gore bus trip (–)
July 30	Advertisement placed in national papers calling for Quayle to step down from the ticket (–)
August 5-7	Second Clinton/Gore bus trip (–)
August 13	Baker resigns as Secretary of State to become Bush's Chief of Staff and to direct the campaign (+)
September 4	Clinton says he knew about his uncle's role in helping him avoid the draft (+)
September 10	Bush gives economic address in Detroit (+)
September 16	First debate canceled (–)
September 19	Crowe endorses Clinton (–)
September 21	Bush attacks Clinton's draft record as new information comes out (+)
September 29	Bush makes debate proposal (+)
October 14	State Department admits error in passport probe (–)

SOURCES: *Facts on File* (1984, 1988, 1992); Moore (1986); Runkel (1989); Goldman, Mathews, et al. (1989); Goldman, Fuller, et al. (1985).

variable, events are given a score of 0 for all days up to and including the day of the event, and then a score of +1 or –1 for all days after the event occurred, depending on whether they are expected to have a positive or negative effect on the Republican candidate. The events are then summed across the days of the campaign. For example, in 1984 the events variable had a score of 0 up through June 6, when Mondale won the California primary and claimed the Democratic nomination. In response to this event, the events variable took on a score of –1 from June 7 through June 12, when Mondale announced the beginning of his vice presidential candidate search. Following this event, the events variable took on a value of –2 and changed back to –1 on June 15 in response to Reagan's June 14 announcement that he was willing to meet with the Soviets. Reagan is expected to have lost support in response to the first two events and gained support in response to the last event.

One potential problem with a variable such as this is that it captures only the effect of events on the national standing of the candidates. As Shaw (1995) points out, campaign events can serve other purposes, such as influencing opinion in certain states, positioning a candidate for the long run, or inoculating the candidate against some future attack. All of these things may pay dividends to the candidate that do not manifest themselves in relatively coterminous shifts in national opinion. However, given that the events included in this analysis are among the most highly visible events in the campaign, it is entirely reasonable to expect the events tally variable to have an effect on changes in candidate support during the campaign period.

That the events tally variable fits quite well with the on-line information processing perspective described in Chapter 3 is no accident. As events unfold, voters update the information they have about candidates and use this information to shape their evaluations of the candidates until the next event occurs. At that time, voters are provided with more information and they reshape their evaluations of the candidates.

MOMENTUM

Another rather elusive influence on candidate success is momentum. *Momentum* effects, also known as *bandwagon* effects, occur when increases (or decreases) in a candidate's poll standing, perhaps as a result of a campaign event, generate even more (or less) support for the candidate. In short, success generates more success. Not much is known about momentum in general election contests. Most of the existing research on momentum is based on small-sample experimental studies and has produced mixed results (Traugott 1992). Most of what we know about momentum in real-world contests is based on research on presidential primary elections. Bartels (1988) has found that momentum is a key variable in explaining success in the primary election process. In primary elections, momentum translates into viability, which translates into increased media attention and increased fund-raising ability. General elections, however, are different from primary elections. First, in primary elections momentum is gained by winning early primaries and generating attention and support for later primaries. In the general election campaign, however, there are no early elections that can generate momentum for later elections—there is just one election day. In general elections, momentum is gained not from early election victories but from doing well, or at least better than expected, in trial-heat public opinion polls. Another difference between primaries and general elections is that primaries often involve several candidates, many of whom are relatively unknown to the voters. Most general election campaigns, however, involve two major party candidates about whom voters usually have more information than they do about primary candidates. Because information about candidates is scarcer in primary elections, it is reasonable to assume that the information generated by increased media coverage is more important to primary voters than to general election voters.

Although they are different from primaries, it is expected that similar but perhaps less pronounced momentum effects exist in general election campaigns. Skalaban (1988) found that paying attention to poll results had a significant influence on voting behavior during the 1980 election. According to Skalaban, those voters who paid attention to the polls in September 1980, when Reagan was ahead in most polls, were more likely to vote for Reagan than those who did not pay attention to the polls. Nadeau, Niemi, and Amato (1994) also found that voter expectations about who would win had a significant influence on party support in British general elections. To date, however, there are no studies of the effect of momentum in U.S. presidential general election campaigns.

One basis for expecting significant momentum effects is offered by Nadeau et al.: ". . . some voters respond to the implicit bonus of being on the winning side" (1994, 378). All else held equal, voting for a winning candidate appears to offer some value for some voters. As poll results are reported in the media, voters incorporate them as one more piece of information when evaluating the relative merits of the candidates. This, of course, assumes that poll results or information about the likely winner is readily available to voters. Indeed, there is substantial circumstantial evidence to support this proposition. In 1992, for instance, in the period between the end of the conventions and election day, over 100 national trial-heat polls were conducted for major national print and television media outlets (The American Enterprise 1992, 100-101). This figure does not include the number of polls taken during the summer of 1992. In addition, during the general election campaign of 1992, 27% of all campaign stories on the ABC, CBS, and NBC evening news programs focused on the "horse race" aspect of the campaign (Stanley and Niemi 1994, 63). Clearly, there are many opportunities for voters to become aware of the competitive nature of the race.

Another possible explanation for momentum effects lies not in the value voters place on supporting a winner but in the way political and media elites react to poll numbers. First, it is possible that potential campaign contributors will feel more comfortable if they think they are betting on a winner and be more forthcoming with contributions that might strengthen the campaign. Perhaps more important, however, is the way the media respond to poll results. There is some tendency for the media to treat candidates differently depending on their standing in the polls. Patterson (1989), for instance, found that the amount of favorable media coverage of Bush and Dukakis in 1988 was positively related to their relative standing in the polls during the general election campaign. Positive press coverage translates into positive information being conveyed to the voters, which should lead to more improvement in the polls.

Good poll numbers, then, may influence voters directly or indirectly. Whatever the mechanism, it is expected that momentum plays a role in the dynamics of general election campaigns. In this analysis the effect of momentum is captured with a variable that measures the change in candidate support in public opinion polls over a relatively short period of time. Specifically, for every day in the analysis, the difference between the Republican estimated polling margin (see Appendix A) on the previous day and the Republican polling margin five days earlier is used to measure short-term change in candidate support. If this number is positive, indicating a Republican gain in support, it should translate into more support for the Republican candidate. If the change is negative, indicating a Republican loss in support, it should translate into a further decline in Republican support. One important point to bear in mind is that momentum does not occur in a vacuum. Public opinion changes in response to campaign events or changes in national conditions; momentum then exacerbates these changes.

National Conditions

According to the hypotheses presented in Chapter 3, national conditions are also expected to play a role in determining candidate support during and across election campaigns. In short, the expectation is that the political and economic context of the election has an effect on the level of candidate support. Specifically, the national political and economic climate is expected to favor either the incumbent party or the challenging party. If voters are relatively satisfied with the current climate, the incumbent party, which represents the status quo, is expected to benefit; if voters are dissatisfied, the challenging party, as the agent of change, should benefit.

NATIONAL POLITICAL AND ECONOMIC CLIMATE

There are two relatively distinct dimensions to the national political and economic climate. One dimension that has received abundant attention in the election forecasting literature (see Chapter 3) is the state of the economy or assessments of the state of the economy. Any number of indicators of the state of the economy can be and have been used in analyses of aggregate election outcomes: specific economic indicators, such as the unemployment rate, growth in income, growth in GNP, and the rate of inflation, or indicators of perceptions of the economy, such as perceived personal finances or perceived national economic conditions. The measure of economic performance used in this analysis is the Index of Consumer Sentiment (ICS). The ICS is a broad measure of public perceptions of the state of the economy. The index is based on a monthly public opinion poll that includes five survey questions that tap into both retrospective and prospective evaluations of the economy.[2] Because high values of the ICS indicate stronger economic performance and because the Republicans held the White House in the years analyzed here, it is anticipated that there should be a positive relationship between the ICS and support for the Republican candidate.

Evaluations of the state of the economy are expected to influence candidate support because they bear directly on evaluations of the incumbent president and level of satisfaction with the current administration. Although economic conditions are an important source of presidential support, there are many other factors voters may use when evaluating the president, such as handling of foreign affairs, personal charisma, positions on specific issues, and the like. In this analysis, presidential popularity is used as a surrogate for the multitude of noneconomic sources of presidential support and any economic sources of support not covered by the ICS. The measure of presidential popularity used here is the percentage of the public that approves of the way the president is handling his job.[3] Because the Republicans held the White House for all three years in this analysis, it is expected that presidential popularity will be positively related to support for the Republican candidate.

Both consumer sentiment and presidential popularity should serve as good measures of the political and economic climate of the country during and across election campaigns. One problem, however, with using both measures is that they are very highly correlated over time. Across the three campaigns studied here, the correlation between consumer sentiment and presidential popularity is .96, indicating that they both tend to move in the same direction. Collinearity of this magnitude can pose severe problems for statistical analysis (Lewis-Beck 1986). One mechanism for avoiding this problem is to combine both variables into a single indicator of the political and economic climate. Because the two variables are measured on different scales (popularity is measured as a percentage and consumer sentiment is an index with a base of 100), they have to be standardized before they can be combined into a single variable. The standardization procedure used here is very simple: Each observation of each variable is expressed as a percentage of the highest value of that variable (59.9 for popularity and 100.9 for consumer sentiment) during the three campaign periods examined here. The index of national conditions is then created by calculating the average of the two standardized variables for each day of the analysis. This average, then, represents the national political and economic climate. Consider the following example. If on a given day presidential popularity value is 45 (75.1% of the highest popularity value) and the ICS is 82 (81.3% of the maximum ICS value), the combined index would equal 78.2 (the average of 75.1 and 81.3). If on another day presidential popularity is at 54 and the ICS is at 90, the overall index is equal to 89.7, indicating that on average the two variables are 89.7% of their maximum values. The incumbent party candidate would be expected to be in a better position on the latter day than on the former.

EXTERNAL EVENTS

In addition to the state of the economy and presidential popularity, it is possible that events occurring in the national or international political arena might spill over into the presidential campaign. In other words, events occurring outside the campaign might have an influence on the standing of the candidates. For example, if some type of international incident or crisis involving the United States occurs, it is possible that voters will rally around the president, which might benefit the incumbent party presidential candidate. On the other hand, if a scandal involving members of the administration were to occur, it is possible that the incumbent party candidate could be hurt in the court of public opinion. The logic of this argument is largely the same as that used in the earlier discussion of the role of subordinate campaign events. As external events occur they provide voters with information that can be incorporated into evaluations of the parties and candidates.

All external events used in the analysis are listed in Table 6.2. These events generally fall into three different categories: international crises, international diplomacy, and scandal. External events are operationalized in the same manner as campaign events. Events are given a score of 0 for all days up to and including the day of the event and a score of +1 or −1 for all days

Table 6.2   Important External Events, 1984-1992

1984
September 7	Meese nomination set aside (–)
September 11	Gromyko invited to U.S. (+)
September 20	U.S. embassy in Beirut bombed (+)
September 24	Reagan addresses United Nations (+)
September 27	Mondale meets Gromyko (–)
September 28	Reagan meets with Gromyko (+)
October 1	Labor secretary Donovan indicted (–)

1988
June 14	Pentagon scandal announced (–)
June 10	Investigation of Jim Wright announced (+)
June 19-21	Reagan at economic summit (+)
July 3	U.S. shoots down Iranian airliner (+)
July 5	Meese announces he will resign (–)
July 12	Thornburgh announced as Meese replacement (+)
July 18	Justice Dept. announces that Meese "probably violated the law" (–)

1992
June 16	Weinberger indicted (–)
June 16-17	Bush and Yeltsin hold D.C. summit (+)
July 6-8	Bush at Munich Economic Summit (+)
August 25	Schultz's notes, suggesting that Bush knew about the arms-for-hostages deal, are made public (–)
August 26	"No-Fly" zone established in Iraq (+)
September 1	Bush addresses nation (Hurricane Andrew) (+)
October 7	NAFTA signed (+)
October 30	Weinberger notes, indicating that Bush was involved in Iran-Contra, are released (–)

SOURCES: *Facts on File* (1984, 1988, 1992); Moore (1986); Runkel (1989); Goldman, Mathews, et al. (1989); Goldman, Fuller, et al. (1985).

after the event occurs. All external event variables are then summed into a single events tally variable.

A Model of Candidate Support in Presidential Campaigns

The hypotheses presented in Chapter 3 and the evidence amassed in the other chapters provide the foundation for a model of candidate support during and across election campaigns. The model quite simply states that candidate support during presidential election campaigns is a function of two categories of influence: campaign events and national conditions. These two groups of variables do not, however, influence candidate support in the same manner. Campaign events are seen as exerting primary influence over changes in candidate support *during* presidential campaigns. In other words, changes in candidate support between June and November of an election year are most likely going to be in response to the occurrence of campaign events. National conditions are expected to play a less decisive role in explaining changes in candidate support during an election campaign than across campaigns. This expectation is based on the fact that national conditions are not likely to change drastically over a few months. Instead, it is expected that the national political and economic climate is fairly constant during a campaign season. National conditions do vary, quite widely in fact, across campaign periods, and it is here that they are expected to have the greatest influence. Together, national conditions and campaign events are expected to explain variations in candidate support during and across the campaign period. In doing so, it is suggested that both factors play a role in determining the eventual outcome.

Analysis of Model

The analysis of this model uses data shown in earlier chapters: trial-heat poll results from early June through election day for the 1984, 1988, and 1992 elections. These data (see Figure 3.6 in Chapter 3) document the ebb and flow of candidate support during the three general election campaign periods. The dependent variable is the daily Republican percentage point advantage over the Democratic candidate. Positive values of the dependent variable indicate the Republicans have more support than the Democrats and negative values indicate the opposite. Because the Republicans held the presidency during each of these campaigns, the dependent variable can also be viewed as the advantage the incumbent party holds over the challenging party.

The independent variables in this analysis are intended to capture the separate effects of campaign events and national conditions on candidate support in the three campaign periods. The major campaign influences—conventions and debates—are operationalized with a series of dichotomous variables. For the conventions, a score of 0 is assigned to each day up to and including the first day of the convention, and all days after the opening day are given a score of 1.[4] Similar variables are created for each of the presidential debates:

Each of the debate variables is scored 0 for all days up to and including the day of the debate and 1 for each day following the debate. The coefficients for the convention and debate variables will tell how much change there is in candidate support as a result of these events.

The operational variables for subordinate campaign events, momentum, and national factors are measured as described earlier in this chapter. The only other variable added to the model is a variable to control for Ross Perot's presence in the 1992 race. The analysis in Chapter 5 indicated that Perot's presence may have had a greater deleterious effect on Clinton's standing than on Bush's. To control for this effect, the Perot variable is coded 1 for the period when Perot was in the race, both officially and unofficially, and 0 for the period when he was not.

SOURCES OF CANDIDATE SUPPORT
DURING PRESIDENTIAL CAMPAIGNS

The first part of the analysis concentrates on the role of the independent variables in explaining changes in candidate support within each of the three campaigns. The results of this analysis, presented in Table 6.3, provide strong support for the model. Overall, the model does a very capable job of explaining variation in the dependent variable in each of the three election years, producing R^2 statistics of .58 for 1984, .78 for 1988, and .79 for 1992. In addition to providing strong explanatory capacity, the overwhelming majority of the coefficients in the model are statistically significant and in the anticipated direction.

Campaign Variables

As expected, each of the six conventions had a significant effect on candidate support. The coefficients for these variables represent the bump in support for the convening party over the remainder of the campaign, controlling for other influences. Sometimes the convention bump was fairly modest, such as for both conventions in 1984 (2.81- and 4.01-point bumps) and the 1988 Democratic convention (3.86-point bump); but other times the convention bump was quite substantial, such as for the 1988 Republican convention (7.55-point bump) and the 1992 Democratic convention (10.32-point bump). These values are somewhat different from those presented earlier in Chapter 4, but some differences are to be expected because different methods are used to calculate the size of the bumps.

Table 6.3   Determinants of Candidate Support During Presidential Campaigns, 1984-1992 (GLS Results)

	1984	1988	1992
Constant	−32.16	−29.94	−68.28**
	(20.04)	(28.0)	(12.30)
Campaign variables			
Democratic convention	−2.81**	−3.86**	−10.32**
	(.66)	(1.29)	(1.70)
Republican convention	4.01**	7.55**	5.03**
	(.93)	(1.53)	(1.22)
First debate	−3.15**	−1.98	−2.13
	(1.01)	(1.33)	(1.76)
Second debate	3.36**	2.64**	−2.27
	(1.03)	(1.25)	(1.90)
Third debate	—	—	2.25
	—	—	(1.77)
Campaign events	−.28	1.86**	.59
	(.25)	(.33)	(.39)
Momentum	.26**	.14**	.17**
	(.05)	(.06)	(.06)
Perot	—	—	7.23**
	—	—	(1.18)
National variables			
External events	1.21**	.94	−.34
	(.49)	(.78)	(.73)
Political and economic environment	.48**	.28	.93**
	(.22)	(.32)	(.17)
R^2	.58	.78	.79
SE	1.78	1.79	2.01
N	149	148	150

NOTE: Results estimated using the Yule-Walker procedure, which corrected for first-order autocorrelation (.38, .62, .59, for 1984, 1988, and 1992, respectively). Standard errors are in parentheses.
*$p < .10$; **$p < .05$.

The results in Table 6.3 also indicate that debates have a similar but less important effect on candidate support. In two of the three years, at least one debate had a significant influence on candidate support. In 1984, the debates had almost equal, offsetting effects on candidate support, with Mondale gaining slightly more than three points from the first debate and Reagan gaining slightly more from the second debate. In 1988, the first debate did not produce a significant change in candidate support but Bush gained almost three points from the second debate. Contrary to what was found in Chapter 5, it is notable that the third debate in 1992 did not have any significant effect on candidate support. Recall that in Chapter 5 it was found that George Bush actually gained support following the third debate, even though Clinton was seen as the "winner" of the debate. At the time it was suggested that this anomalous effect was probably due to the increase in Perot's level of support, primarily at Clinton's expense. When a control variable for Perot's presence is included in the multivariate model, there is no apparent effect from the third debate.

The evidence in Table 6.3 is mixed with regard to the effect of other campaign events. In both 1984 and 1992, there is no evidence that other campaign events had a significant effect on candidate support. In 1988, however, the results indicate that debates and conventions may not be the only events that matter during presidential campaigns. Instead, the vast array of subordinate campaign events can also have an effect on candidate support. In 1988, the occurrence of these types of events produced changes in candidate support on the order of approximately 1.86 percentage points. Although this variable was significant only in one year, this finding provides some indication of how important it can be for campaigns to exercise control over what happens during the campaign.

Momentum also appears to be an influential factor in general election campaigns. According to the results in Table 6.3, momentum was a significant influence on candidate support in each of the three years and was particularly important in 1984. Based on these findings it appears that when the polls turn in a candidate's favor there is a natural tendency to pick up extra support based on short-term gains in the polls.

Finally, it appears that Perot's presence in the 1992 race did more than just suppress the anomalous effect of the third debate—it also had a pronounced effect on the pattern of support for Bush and Clinton. The coefficient for this variable indicates that when Perot was in the race, Bush's relative standing was approximately 7.23 percentage points higher than when Perot was out of the race. This is very much in keeping with the evidence presented in Chapter 5 that showed a clear trade-off between Clinton and Perot support.

National Variables

In addition to the campaign variables, the results for the national variables are generally as expected. First, the evidence from the external events variable is very mixed. Only in 1984 does it appear that external events had a significant influence on candidate support. In 1984, external events, on average, created changes in candidate support of approximately 1.21 percentage points. Some of the more visible external events in 1984 were the bombing of the U.S. embassy in Beirut, Gromyko's visit to the United States, and the indictment of Secretary of Labor Ray Donovan. In 1988 and 1992, however, there is no evidence that external events had a significant influence on candidate support even though some were ostensibly just as important as events in 1984 (e.g., Weinberger's indictment and revelations in Shultz's and Weinberger's notes indicating a substantial Bush involvement in the Iran-Contra affair).

The effect of the political and economic climate was more consistent, although the results are still mixed. In both 1984 and 1992, there is strong evidence that changes in presidential popularity and consumer sentiment had a significant effect on candidate support. This effect is particularly pronounced in 1992, where the coefficient (.93) is almost twice the size of the coefficient for 1984 (.48). The effect of national conditions during campaigns was expected to be determined somewhat by the degree to which national conditions varied during the campaigns. The results in Table 6.3 bear this out: The standard deviation for the national conditions variable was greatest during the 1992 campaign (2.8), then the 1984 campaign (1.9), and lowest for the 1988 campaign (1.8). What these results suggest is that when national conditions change substantially they can have an effect on changes in candidate support during an election campaign.

SOURCES OF CANDIDATE SUPPORT
DURING AND ACROSS PRESIDENTIAL CAMPAIGNS

The preceding results comport very nicely with the expectations of the model. Campaign events, especially the major campaign events, exert considerable influence on changes in candidate support during presidential campaigns. National conditions also have some effect on candidate support, especially when they exhibit variation during the campaign season. But the real objective of the model is not just to explain variation in candidate support during the campaign, but also to explain variation in support for candidates across campaigns. It is here, in explaining variation across campaigns, that national conditions are expected to exert the greatest influence. For example, whereas changes in national conditions had very little to do with changes in candidate support during the 1988 campaign, it is expected that national conditions played a major role in determining the overall level of candidate support in the 1988 campaign compared to other years. When focusing on the within-year analysis there is no appropriate way to test hypotheses such as this.

To analyze the general effects of campaign events and national conditions on candidate support, the trial-heat data from the 1984, 1988, and 1992 elections are pooled together to form a single data set. Pooling the data in this manner creates the potential for certain statistical problems that do not usually exist in a simple time series analysis (Stimson 1985). In particular, the most serious problem for this analysis is the possible existence of unique intercepts (unit effects) for each year. These unit effects, should they exist, would be indicative of some peculiar aspect of each year that has not been incorporated into the models. To ameliorate this problem, two dummy variables are added to the model, one representing the 1984 campaign and one representing the 1988 campaign.[5]

The analysis of candidate support during and across campaigns is presented in Table 6.4 where, with the exception of the inclusion of the 1984 and 1988 dummy variables, all variables are the same as in Table 6.3 (see Appendix C for alternative formulations of the model). In many ways, the findings in Table 6.4 mirror those in Table 6.3. First, the R^2 statistic (.88) and the standard error (1.88) once again suggest that the model bears a striking resemblance to reality. In fact, the fit of the pooled model is closer than for any of the single-year models presented in Table 6.3. Second, most of the coefficients are very similar to what they were in the within-year analysis. There are, of course, certain important exceptions. The pooled analysis, for instance, finds a stronger convention bump for the Republicans in 1988 than was found in the within-year analysis (10.98 versus 7.55). Also, the within-year analysis found a significant debate bump for Mondale following the first debate in 1984, but such an effect is not indicated in the pooled analysis.

Beyond these major-event effects, the results of the pooled analysis allow for general conclusions concerning the effects of other variables: subordinate events, momentum, and national conditions. Although they were significant in only one year (1988) in the within-year analysis, subordinate campaign

Table 6.4   A Pooled Model of Candidate Support Within and Across Election Years, 1984-1992 (GLS Results)

Variable	b	t-*Score*
Constant	−58.18	−6.49**
Conventions		
Democratic, 1984	−2.43	−2.44**
Republican, 1984	3.81	3.78**
Democratic, 1988	−4.64	−4.31**
Republican, 1988	10.98	8.94**
Democratic, 1992	−10.99	−7.66**
Republican, 1992	4.67	4.63**
Debates		
First, 1984	−.78	−.64
Second, 1984	4.19	3.08**
First, 1988	.88	.74
Second, 1988	4.06	3.32**
First, 1992	−2.52	−1.56
Second, 1992	−2.20	−1.26
Third, 1992	2.47	1.50
Perot	6.76	6.49**
Campaign events	.78	3.96**
Momentum	.17	5.35**
National variables		
External events	.25	.63
Political and economic climate	.79	6.34**
Year effects		
1984	−.01	−.004
1988	−19.12	−6.91**

NOTE: The data have been corrected for first-order autocorrelation using the Yule-Walker procedure. The estimated value of first-order autocorrelation (prior to correction) is .59.
$R^2 = .88$; $SE = 1.88$; $N = 446$.
*$p < .10$; **$p < .05$.

events have a general effect in the pooled analysis, producing changes in candidate support on the order of .78 percentage points when they occur. This is considerably less than the effect demonstrated for the 1988 campaign in Table 6.3, but may still be considered an important source of support for candidates in close elections. Certainly, the ability to control the flow of these events could prove to be a valuable asset to any campaign.

The general effect of momentum over these three elections is a gain of .17 percentage points for every percentage point improvement in the polls in the previous four days. For example, if a candidate gained 6 percentage points on his foe over a four-day period due to some campaign event, he or she would have gained 7.02 percentage points by the fifth day—the original 6 points plus 1.02 points (6 points × .17)—due to momentum. Over the course of a campaign, momentum could prove to be an important asset toward keeping the trend in opinion going in the right direction.

Finally, national conditions play a critical role in helping to shape candidate support across the campaigns studied here. Although the external events do not significantly affect candidate support, the prevailing national political and economic climate has a clear, strong, and positive influence on the fortunes of the candidates across the 1984, 1988, and 1992 campaigns. However, because the coefficient is based on a standardized variable, its effect is difficult to interpret. By comparing the differences in national conditions across two campaigns in which these conditions differed drastically (1984 and 1992), and the effect these differences produced on candidate support, it is possible to gain an appreciation for the impact of this variable. During the 1984 campaign, the average popularity rating was 55.2 and the average for the Index of Consumer Sentiment was 97.7, whereas in 1992 the average popularity rating was 36.0 and the average Index of Consumer Sentiment was 76.5. These values of popularity and consumer confidence produce national conditions index values of 94.5 for 1984 and 68.0 for 1992. Clearly, national conditions favored Ronald Reagan much more than they did George Bush. Based only on the difference in national conditions (94.5 − 68.0 = 26.5), support for Reagan during the 1984 campaign is predicted to be 20.9 points higher (26.5 × .79) than for Bush during the 1992 campaign. Clearly, national conditions play a critical role in determining the level of support for candidates across election years.

The pooled model, then, offers many of the same conclusions reached in the within-year analysis: A wide variety of campaign events—conventions, debates, subordinate events, momentum, the Perot candidacy—have an effect on candidate support in presidential election campaigns. In addition, the pooled model makes clear how important national conditions are, not only in explaining candidate support during campaigns but especially in explaining different levels of candidate support across campaigns. The combination of these effects in the pooled model produces a highly accurate statistical explanation of candidate support in presidential campaigns. Figure 6.1 provides a clear depiction of the accuracy of the model across the three campaigns. As can plainly be seen, predicted values of candidate support

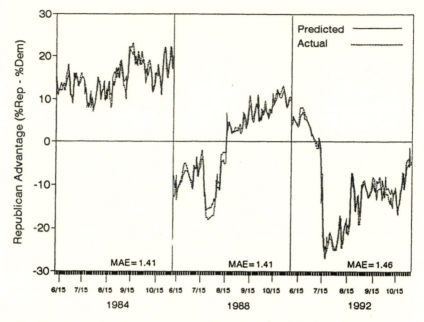

Figure 6.1. Actual and Predicted Levels of Candidate Support, 1984-1992

follow the same course as the actual values and rarely stray very far from this course. The mean absolute error (MAE) does not exceed 1.46 percentage points in any of the three years, which means that, on average, the predicted values are no more than 1.46 percentage points from the observed values. There can be little doubt that, except perhaps for a few minor deviations, the model of candidate support in presidential campaigns presented here captures quite well the important elements of campaign politics.

RELATIVE IMPORTANCE

This book began with a discussion of the tension between two schools of thought concerning the effect of campaigns and national conditions on election outcomes. Specifically, the dominant view is that election outcomes are easily predicted without any reference to the presidential campaign; therefore, campaigns do not appear to matter. The alternative perspective, however, holds that the sound and fury of presidential campaigns are central to gaining a clear understanding of election outcomes. In fact, the analysis in this and the earlier chapters has illustrated that campaigns do matter—they are central determinants of changes in candidate support during the campaign and, therefore, contribute to the election outcome. In particular, the multivariate analysis in this chapter makes it clear that campaign events, especially the major events, hold considerable sway over public opinion. Of course, this analysis also finds the same to be true for national conditions: Candidate support—especially support across campaigns—is heavily influenced by the prevailing political and economic climate. Because both sets of factors influence candidate support, it can be said that election outcomes are jointly produced by campaign events and national conditions.

Although campaign events and national conditions both influence candidate support and, therefore, election outcomes, they are not necessarily equally important in determining outcomes. The concept of relative effect can have many different meanings, however, and can be difficult to measure. One way of illustrating the relative effect of campaign variables and national conditions on election outcomes is presented in Table 6.5. The first two lines in Table 6.5 represent estimates of the aggregate effect of the two groups of variables on candidate support on the last day of polling. Last-day polling results are used here as a proxy for the actual election outcomes (recall from Appendix A that the last-day polling results are very close to the actual election outcome). These estimates are derived by multiplying the value of the independent variables by their respective coefficients and then summing the products for the groups of variables. The resulting numbers represent the net effect of the two categories of variables on candidate support on the last day of polling. When the numbers in Table 6.5 are added to the intercept and year dummy variable coefficients in Table 6.4, the sum should be approximately equal to the predicted value of the dependent variable on the last day of polling.[6] According to these figures, national conditions have a more decisive effect on election outcomes than do campaign variables. In each of the three years, national conditions contribute much more to the election outcome than do campaign events. This is not to say that campaign events have no effect, only that the effect of national conditions is substantially larger.

Other evidence of the effect of national conditions is presented in the last two rows of Table 6.5, which simulate how the three elections would have turned out differently under a different set of national conditions. The simulation is based on the levels of presidential popularity (32%) and

Table 6.5   Net Impact of Campaigns and National Conditions on Candidate
Support in Presidential Elections, 1984-1992

Variable	1984	1988	1992
Net effects			
Campaign variables	.72	15.49	−4.39
National conditions	77.20	73.20	59.00
Simulated outcomes			
Outcome under 1980 conditions	−5.86	−10.21	−10.67
Difference between simulated			
outcomes and original estimates	−25.60	−21.35	−7.15

NOTE: The estimates of net effects are based on multiplying the coefficients in Table 6.4 times the values of
the independent variables on the last day of polling and then summing the products. Estimates for the simulated
outcomes are based on simulating 1980 values of presidential popularity (32%) and consumer sentiment (76.7)
for each of the three election years. The resulting number reflects an estimate of the difference between the
Republican and Democratic vote shares in each election year if national conditions had been the same as in 1980.
The numbers in the fourth line are calculated by subtracting the original estimated outcome from the simulated
outcome.

consumer sentiment (76.7) that existed at the time of the 1980 presidential
election. The numbers in the third line of Table 6.5 represent the expected
outcome (Republican percentage minus Democratic percentage) under these
conditions, and the last line represents the difference between the simulated
estimates and the estimates based on the actual national conditions. According to these results, the Republicans would have lost all three elections if
they had been held under 1980 national conditions. Furthermore, the difference between the simulated and original estimates indicate that the simulated
conditions would have cost the Republicans almost 26 percentage points in
1984, 21 percentage points in 1988, and 7 percentage points in 1992.

WHITHER THE CAMPAIGN?

These results do not mean campaigns are irrelevant nor do they negate the
results from the rest of the book, which found campaign variables to be a
significant influence on candidate support. What these results mean is that
although campaigns do matter and are relevant determinants of candidate
support, national conditions carry more weight in determining the eventual
outcome. Although this may seem inconsistent with many of the findings in
the rest of the book, it is not surprising to find modest (relative to national
conditions) campaign effects on election outcomes, especially when mea-

suring effect in the manner used in Table 6.5. After all, the volumes of research on election forecasting are quite clear on one point: National conditions are important determinants of election outcomes.

Another key to understanding the findings in Table 6.5 is that campaigns are (usually) contests between two well-equipped sides, both of which are fighting to keep the other side from gaining the upper hand. One clear possibility is that both sides could put up equally good efforts and the net effect of the campaign could turn out to be zero because each side effectively neutralized the other side. The 1984 campaign represents a good example of this; although the conventions, the second debate, momentum, and other campaign events produced significant effects, the cumulative effect of the campaign was only a slight boost (.72 points) to Reagan's level of support. The 1992 campaign also illustrates this point; although Clinton got an 11-point convention bump, Bush managed to gain most of it back, with the aid of Ross Perot, over the rest of the campaign. In the end, Clinton netted only a 4-percentage-point advantage due to campaign variables, even though there were very substantial shifts in candidate support in response to campaign events. However, because these shifts were in opposite directions—some favoring Clinton, some favoring Bush—they canceled each other out in the end. The 1988 campaign provides an example of asymmetric campaign effects —that is, a case in which the spoils of the campaign were decidedly lopsided. Building on a strong convention bump, Bush managed to net 15 percentage points over Dukakis due to campaign variables. This jibes well with the popular perception that the Bush camp ran a better campaign than the Dukakis camp.

The differences in campaign effects across the years might, then, be indicative of the degree to which the candidates ran relatively balanced campaigns. The irony in this is that two effective, well-run campaigns can appear to have little effect on the election outcome, at least compared to the effect of national conditions. But the analysis in Table 6.5 represents only one way of examining the effects of campaigns on election outcomes. Rather than comparing the effect of campaign events with the effect of national conditions, it may prove useful to analyze the effect of campaign events in isolation and ask if the elections would have turned out differently under alternative campaign scenarios. For instance, in 1992 George Bush gained almost 7 percentage points on Bill Clinton when Ross Perot reentered the race in October. Although the election outcome would have been the same—Clinton winning—Perot's presence in the race clearly changed the meaning of the

Table 6.6   The Impact of Alternative Campaign Scenarios on Presidential
Election Outcomes, 1984-1992

Campaign Scenario	1984 Predicted Outcome	1988 Predicted Outcome	1992 Predicted Outcome
1984 Campaign effects	—	–3.36*	1.54*
1988 Campaign effects	34.51	—	16.31*
1992 Campaign effects	14.62	–8.49*	—

NOTE: All entries represent predicted election outcomes (Republican percentage minus Democratic percentage) based on alternative campaign scenarios. Entries marked with an asterisk represent instances in which the alternative scenario could change the election outcome.

outcome: Instead of winning with a clear majority of the vote, Perot's candidacy doomed Clinton to being a plurality president.

Extending this logic, it is interesting to muse about how all three of the elections studied here would have turned out if the net effects of the campaigns had been different than they actually were. Table 6.6 presents an analysis of the effect of different campaign scenarios on the 1984, 1988, and 1992 election outcomes. These data reflect the election outcomes that would be expected to have occurred from 1984 to 1992 if each election experienced the campaign effects produced by the other two elections. For example, the first number in the first column of data, 34.51, reflects the expected outcome (Republican vote advantage) in 1984 if the 1984 campaign had produced the same net effect produced by the 1988 campaign. Recall from Table 6.5 that the net effect of the 1984 campaign was very small (.72), whereas the net effect of the 1988 campaign was quite substantial (15.49). If these effects had been transposed, the ultimate outcome would have been the same but Reagan would have won by a landslide of truly monumental proportions.

Applying the logic to other elections, it is clear that campaign effects play a key role in determining election outcomes. Although the outcome of the 1984 election remains unchanged regardless of campaign scenarios, the data in Table 6.6 suggest that the 1988 and 1992 election outcomes were very dependent on the campaign effects produced during those years. Under both the 1984 and 1992 campaign scenarios, the Republicans would have lost the presidency in 1988; under the 1984 scenario, the Republicans would have probably squeaked out a close victory in 1992, and under the 1988 scenario they would have breezed to victory in 1992. An important point to understand is that these results illustrate the effect of alternative campaign scenarios, holding national conditions constant.

The data in Table 6.6 represent hypothetical examples of what might have occurred under different circumstances but they make a very important point: The elections turned out the way they did in large part due to the effect of the campaigns. If the campaign effects are altered, the election outcome could very well change. This is especially true for elections that are expected to be very close; in cases such as these, a campaign-induced shift of just a few percentage points could easily alter the outcome. This is not meant to obscure the fact that campaigns play a less central role than national conditions in determining the final outcome, but it should be clear that the effect of campaign events can be strong enough to transform election outcomes. This is especially important because candidates cannot do much to alter national conditions, but they can orchestrate campaign events in an effort to manipulate public opinion.

One other way to assess the effect of campaigns and national conditions is to examine the role both groups of variables play in influencing *changes* in public opinion *during* the campaign. Recall from the hypotheses in Chapter 3 that campaign events are expected to play a more important role than national conditions in moving public opinion over the course of the campaign. The method used here to assess the effect of variables on changes in public opinion during a campaign is very straightforward: The change in the value of the independent variables from the first to the last day of the analysis is multiplied times the respective coefficient for each variable and the products are summed within categories (campaign versus national). The sum of these products, presented in Table 6.7, represents the predicted net effect of campaigns and national conditions on changes in candidate support during the campaign.[7] According to the figures in Table 6.7, the expectations laid out in Chapter 3 are largely confirmed. With the exception of 1984, campaign variables play a much more important role than national conditions in explaining changes in candidate support during the campaign. The effect of national conditions is fairly constant across the three years, moving public opinion only 2.7 percentage points, on average, during the three campaign seasons. The effect of campaign events, on the other hand, is highly variable from one year to the next. In 1984, campaign events were only slightly less influential than national conditions, whereas in 1988 and 1992, campaign events exerted much more influence over changes in candidate support than did national conditions.

Table 6.7   The Net Impact of National Conditions and Campaign Events on Changes in Candidate Support During Presidential Campaigns, 1984-1992

	1984	*1988*	*1992*
National conditions	3.32	2.19	2.61
Campaign events	2.60	17.22	−11.36

NOTE: All entries represent the predicted impact of the groups of variables on changes in candidate support from the beginning to the end of the campaign. These effects are calculated by multiplying the change in the value of each variable from the first to the last days of the analysis times the coefficient of the variable. The sum of these products, within categories, represents the net impact of national conditions and campaign events on changes in candidate support during the campaign periods.

Why did campaign effects have so much influence on changes in candidate support in 1988 and 1992—when they clearly dominated the influence of national conditions—but so little in 1984 that they actually had a weaker influence than national conditions? One possibility was alluded to earlier in this chapter: It may be that the 1984 campaign was relatively balanced, leading to a canceling-out effect, whereas the 1988 and 1992 campaigns were not balanced, possibly generating an advantage for one candidate over the other. Although this is a plausible explanation, it is not possible (at least here) to measure the degree to which the campaigns were or were not balanced.

Another possible explanation for the varying effects of campaigns can be found in the discussion of anticipated campaign effects in Chapter 3. Recall that it was hypothesized that the magnitude of campaign effects would be partially dependent on the difference between the existing level of candidate support and the equilibrium level of support; the greater the disparity between these two levels, the greater the potential for campaign effects. Given this, it might be expected that the net effect of the campaign would be less for those campaigns in which public opinion is relatively in sync with the equilibrium level of candidate support at the beginning of the campaign. In other words, if the level of candidate support early in the campaign coincides with where it is expected to be at the end of the campaign, it is perhaps unlikely that strong campaign effects will emerge because there is little room for movement in mass opinion. The data in Table 6.8 bear this out to some degree. The disparity between opinion early in the campaign and the equilibrium (forecasted) outcome was the greatest in 1988, then 1992, and was the smallest in 1984. The magnitude of net campaign effects (see Table 6.5 and Table 6.7) was also the greatest in 1988, then in 1992, and was

Table 6.8   Disparity Between Early Poll Results and Predicted Election
Outcomes, 1984-1992

	1984	1988	1992
Republican standing early in the campaign	+18.4	−10.3	+5.4
Predicted Republican margin of victory in November	+16.5	+2.3	−5.0
Difference between early standing and predicted outcome	−1.9	+12.6	−10.4

NOTE: The early standing is based on the average of the first seven days of poll results in each of the three years (June 4-10, 1984; June 7-13, 1988; June 2-8, 1992). The predicted outcome is based on the results of the spring forecasting model presented in Chapter 3.

the smallest in 1984. Although these results represent only three election campaigns, they are consistent with the idea that the magnitude of campaign effects is somewhat dependent on the disparity between the expected election outcome and the level of candidate support early in the campaign. These findings point to a complicated interactive relationship between national conditions and presidential campaigns.

Conclusion

The analysis in this chapter supports many of the hypotheses and ideas developed earlier regarding the role of campaigns and national conditions as determinants of candidate support. First, campaigns and national conditions jointly produce fluctuations in candidate support during presidential campaigns and ultimately influence election outcomes. Second, campaign events are primarily responsible for influencing changes in candidate support during the campaign season whereas national conditions are primarily responsible for influencing the general or the equilibrium level of candidate support across campaigns. Third, when focusing on the end game—the election outcome—national conditions are more influential than campaign events, although campaigns do have the potential the alter election outcomes. Fourth, there is evidence to suggest an interaction between campaign effects and national conditions. Specifically, national conditions—or more precisely, the disparity between early poll standing and the expected election outcome—appear to play an important role in determining the potential effect of campaign events on public opinion in a given election year.

Notes

1. Shaw (1995) uses a similar strategy in his analysis of the effect of campaign events.

2. Monthly data for the ICS were provided by the Survey Research Center, University of Michigan. The base (ICS = 100) for the ICS is February 1986. The index of consumer sentiment is created using responses to the following five survey questions: (1) Would you say that you and your family are better off or worse off financially than you were a year ago? (2) Now, looking ahead—do you think that a year from now you and your family will be better off financially, worse off, or just about the same? (3) Now, turning to business conditions in the country as a whole—do you think that during the next twelve months, we'll have good times financially, bad times, or what? (4) Looking ahead, which would you say is more likely—that in the country as a whole, we'll have continuous good times during the next five years or so, or that we will have periods of widespread unemployment, or depression, or what? (5) About the big things people buy for their homes—I mean furniture, home furnishings, refrigerator, stove, television, and things like that—in general, do you think now is a good time or a bad time to buy such household items?

3. The approval data used here are taken from Gallup polls administered during the campaign. In most cases there were a couple of different polls taken during a month. These figures were used for the days that the polls were taken. Approval ratings for days when no polls were taken were estimated by interpolating between the values of days when poll results were available. The approval data for 1984 and 1988 were taken from Edwards and Gallup (1990). The data for 1992 were provided by the Gallup organization.

4. Campbell, Cherry, and Wink (1992) also include a decay component in their analysis of convention bumps. This type of variable is not included here for several reasons. First, including a decay component (a counter variable for the period after the election) introduces a very high level of collinearity, producing tolerances of less than .02. Second, there is not much evidence that support gained by convention bumps decays over time. Campbell et al. found only limited evidence of a decay process (1992, 303). Also, when decay variables are added to the current analysis their coefficients are in the wrong direction as often as they are in the right direction. Third, to the extent that the effect of convention bumps does decay over time, it is expected to do so as a consequence of the changing values of the other variables in the model.

5. The other possible problem is, of course, the potential for autocorrelation. To compensate for the presence of autocorrelation, the data in this analysis are analyzed using the Yule-Walker method, which corrects for first-order autocorrelation. First-order autocorrelation for the pooled time series is .60. After correction, first-order autocorrelation is .19, $D = 1.63$ (the next four lags are .08, .16, .05, .16). According to Hanushek and Jackson (1977, 173), autocorrelations of .20 or less do not pose serious problems. Lewis-Beck (1986, 234) suggests the cutoff point is .30.

6. This statistic is very similar to Achen's "level of importance" statistic (Achen 1982, 72-73), except that Achen's statistic is intended to demonstrate the average effect of the independent variables.

7. The figures in Table 6.7 are different from those presented in Table 6.5 due to a difference in calculation. Table 6.7 is based on changes in the variables during the campaign, whereas Table 6.5 is based on the value of the independent variables at the end of the campaign.

The Role of Campaigns in U.S. Presidential Elections

This book represents an effort to unearth and describe the role campaigns play in U.S. presidential elections. Although most of the preceding analysis has focused primarily on the 1984, 1988, and 1992 elections, evidence from other years was also brought to bear on the issue. Although much of what was previously known about elections suggests otherwise, the sum total of the evidence suggests an interesting and important role for campaigns.

Part of the problem with understanding the role of campaigns has been that what is known about the importance of presidential campaigns is largely based on studies that do not directly address the role of campaigns in elections. Instead, the existing body of literature suggests that because voting behavior and election outcomes are easily explained by other variables, campaigns must not be important. The problem is that campaign effects are unlikely to be found by analyzing only ultimate vote decisions or election outcomes. A political campaign must be understood to be a process that generates a product, the election outcome, and like any other process, one cannot expect to understand the process by analyzing only the product. This book has tried to further the understanding of the role of campaigns by focusing on both election outcomes and the process that generates them.

A Recapitulation of Hypotheses
and Supporting Evidence

As a means of summarizing the role of campaigns, it is useful to review the major hypotheses developed in Chapter 3 and the degree to which they are supported by the evidence. The first hypothesis acknowledged the important role of national conditions in the campaign process.

> H1: There exists an equilibrium level of candidate support during presidential campaigns and this level of support is a function of exogenous (noncampaign) national political and economic variables.

This hypothesis is supported in many different parts of the preceding analysis. The graphic display of candidate support across campaigns presented in Figure 3.6 clearly showed that the level of candidate support shifts considerably from one election year to the next, suggesting that there may be a different equilibrium level of support for each year. This equilibrium level is thought to be something like the predicted election outcomes generated by the forecasting model in Chapter 2. The pooled campaign analysis in Chapter 6 also supports the idea of a shifting equilibrium. The pooled campaign analysis demonstrated that presidential popularity and consumer sentiment are crucial to explaining differences in candidate support across campaigns.

The second and third hypotheses addressed the determinants of changes in candidate support during single campaign seasons.

> H2: During the campaign season public opinion will deviate, sometimes widely, from the equilibrium level of candidate support. Variations in candidate support during the campaign season are largely attributable to the occurrence of campaign events.
>
> H3: There are rarely significant changes in national political and economic conditions during the campaign; therefore, national conditions have very little effect on changes in public opinion during the campaign.

The data reveal that public opinion does vary, sometimes widely, during campaign periods, and that variations in candidate support are closely tied to the occurrence of campaign events. The analysis in Chapters 4 and 5 documents the effect of the major campaign events, conventions and debates, on candidate support. Conventions in particular were found to have a clear and sometimes pronounced effect on candidate support, whereas debates had a less consistent but sometimes still significant effect. These findings were buttressed by the analysis in Chapter 6, which demonstrates the significant effect of two other campaign variables, subordinate campaign events and momentum, on changes in candidate support during the campaign.

Somewhat contrary to expectations, national conditions also play a role in shaping public opinion during the campaign period. However, the effect of national conditions on changes in candidate support clearly is secondary to the effect of campaign events. National conditions had a mixed effect on changes in candidate support in the within-year analysis presented in Chapter 6. In the pooled analysis, however, the net effect of campaign variables on changes in candidate support was many times greater than the net effect of national conditions. The only exception to this was the 1984 campaign, in which national conditions were slightly more important than campaign events in determining changes in candidate support.

The fourth hypothesis suggested that there may be some interaction between national conditions and the potential effect of campaign events.

H4: The magnitude of the effect of campaign events on public opinion during the campaign is partially dependent on the disparity between the level of support for the candidate at the time of the event and the expected election outcome. Specifically, the greater the negative disparity (running behind the expected level of support), the greater the potential effect of a positive campaign event.

Although this hypothesis is difficult to convincingly confirm, it does find support in the data. First, the analysis of convention bumps in Chapter 4 demonstrates that candidates are likely to be the recipients of relatively large convention bumps if their preconvention level of support is significantly lower than their expected level of support. On the other hand, candidates whose preconvention level of support is very close to or exceeds their expected level of support are likely to received substantially smaller convention bumps. The fourth hypothesis is also supported by the analysis in Chapter 6, which found that the net effect of campaign events appears to be related to the degree to which opinion early in the campaign is out of equilibrium. Campaigns had the greatest effect on changes in candidate support when early public opinion polls deviated substantially from the expected election outcome.

Underlying these hypotheses is the role of information in the campaign process. As the campaign unfolds and events occur, their potential for affecting voters is a function of whether or not voters receive information about the events. If voters receive the information, then a shift in public opinion can be expected as voters update their running tally of candidate evaluations. Most voters are unlikely to receive campaign information directly from the campaign. Instead, the mass media act as the conduit through which voters receive campaign messages.

The analysis in Chapter 3 found a distinct pattern to campaign coverage by the media. Relatively little information is conveyed in the early summer when the level of campaign activity is fairly low. Then, during the convention period, there are large spikes in the amount of campaign information available; the amount of information generated during this period is usually unmatched during any other point in the campaign. Following the conventions there is a decline in information levels until the fall campaign heats up and then there is an increasing amount of information available as the campaign progresses toward election day.

The fifth hypothesis suggested that the effect of campaign events may be in part a function of the value of information at the time the event occurs.

> H5: Because the value of information declines as the cumulative amount of information increases, events that occur early in the campaign period have greater potential to influence voters than do events of equivalent quality that occur later in the campaign.

This hypothesis finds support in a number of different places. First, the convention analysis showed that in any given year the party holding the first convention usually gets a larger bump than the party holding the second convention. Although it is difficult to prove, it is suggested that this is due to the fact that the information produced by the first convention is more valuable to voters than the information produced by the second convention. The findings from the debate analysis in Chapter 5 are also somewhat consistent with the fifth hypothesis. One explanation given for the fact that debates are generally not as influential as conventions is that debates are held toward the end of the campaign when information is less valuable and therefore less likely to produce dramatic results.

The Campaign Process

The campaign process, then, begins with a national context within which the campaign is conducted. This context reflects prevailing attitudes toward the economy and the incumbent administration. The context of the campaign determines the equilibrium outcome, which is the outcome that might be expected to occur given prevailing national conditions. From one election to the next, as the equilibrium outcome changes there are corresponding changes in the overall level of candidate support.

But candidate support at the beginning of the campaign is frequently out of equilibrium; that is to say, it does not match up well with the expected outcome. One of the important roles of the campaign is to help move public opinion toward the expected outcome. As events unfold and voters update their evaluations, public opinion gravitates toward the equilibrium level. One reasonable but not clearly testable hypothesis is that as voters receive the information generated by campaign events they become more informed about the choice before them, which makes their preferences more reflective of prevailing national conditions (Gelman and King 1993).

Some events, of course, are much more important than others in this process, and this is largely a function of the amount and timing of the information generated by the events. Nominating conventions in particular are very important in moving public opinion in the early part of the campaign. Nominating conventions produce large, biased amounts of information at a point in the campaign when it is most useful to voters. Changes in national conditions during the campaign also play some role in moving public opinion but not nearly as important a role as campaign events.

On election day, outcomes are produced that are relatively proximate to what could be expected based on prevailing national conditions. The outcomes themselves are very consistent with the idea that elections are easily predicted with just a few noncampaign variables and, therefore, campaigns have little to do with the outcome. The analysis presented here, however, although recognizing the prominent role of national conditions, illustrates that the election outcome is really jointly produced by the campaign and national conditions.

The first chapter of this book began with a comparison of three different perspectives on the relative importance of campaigns. The first perspective held that it is the campaign that is primarily responsible for determining election outcomes. The second perspective suggested that, although campaigns might have some influence, their effect is really limited by the political and economic context of the election. The third perspective viewed campaigns as nearly or completely irrelevant. According to this view, election outcomes are so heavily influenced by national conditions that it is unlikely that campaigns can do much to change the predestined outcome.

The evidence presented in this book supports something similar to the second viewpoint. Campaigns do matter; they play a very important role in shaping public opinion during an election year and they contribute to the ultimate outcome. But at the same time it is important to recognize that the political and economic context of the election can place parameters on the potential effect of the campaign. Consider the 1984 campaign, for instance. Given the levels of consumer sentiment and presidential popularity in 1984, it was unlikely that even a very poorly run Reagan campaign and a well-run Mondale campaign could do much to alter the expected outcome, a Reagan victory. On the other hand, the outcomes of the 1988 and 1992 elections could have been changed if the net effects of the campaigns had been substantially different. Although George Bush, in 1988, and Bill Clinton, in 1992, owe much of their electoral success to the national context of the elections, their victories also depended on the relatively lopsided effect of the campaign in both years.

Perhaps one way to think about the effect of campaigns relative to national conditions is to think of election outcomes as similar to the outcome of a sporting event such as a basketball game. When teams have star players (say, Glenn Robinson) who habitually pour in twenty to thirty points a game, it is easy to conclude that games are won or lost due to the performance of these star players. On the other hand, it is not unheard of to have a reserve player (say, Marty Conlon) come into games and dish out a few assists, sink important foul shots, or hit a couple of jump shots at crucial points during the game. Although the performance of marquee players no doubt contributes more to the final score, the play of the reserves can provide the points that swing games one way or the other. A similar conclusion applies to campaigns and national conditions: Although national conditions set the parameters of likely outcomes and contribute more to the eventual outcome, campaigns can provide the votes that swing the outcome one way or the other. In years when national conditions overwhelmingly favor one candidate over another, it is unlikely, barring the total collapse of one side of the campaign, that campaigns can provide enough swing to alter the expected outcome. However, in years when the expected outcome is not so lopsided, campaigns may have enough influence to play a critical role in determining the outcome.

Appendix A

Calculating Aggregate Candidate Support

The dependent variable for the aggregate candidate support analysis is based on trial-heat poll results for the race between the major-party presidential candidates. For the 1984 election, the data were taken from Goldman, Fuller, et al. (1985, 454). Goldman, Fuller, et al. present daily tracking poll results provided by Richard Wirthlin, pollster for the Reagan campaign. The poll results are based on four-day tracking polls from June 4 through October 4, and two-day tracking polls from October 5 through November 5. These data are unique compared to those used for the 1988 and 1992 analysis because they are provided by a single polling organization and cover virtually every day from early June through election day.

Gathering the data for 1988 and 1992 required a bit more creativity. These opinion estimates were generated on the basis of poll results provided in

Table A.1   Calculating Candidate Support (in percentages)

	Gallup	*Washington Post/ ABC News*	*Daily Mean*	*Republican Advantage*
June 6				
Bush	31	30	30.5	
Clinton	25	26	25.5	+5
June 7				
Bush	31	30	30.5	
Clinton	25	26	25.5	+5
June 8				
Bush	31	—	31	
Clinton	25	—	25	+6

Public Opinion (November/December, 1988) and *Public Perspective* (July/ August, September/October, and November/December, 1992). Daily candidate support figures were calculated in the following manner. First, poll results for support for the Republican and Democratic candidates were recorded for each day a poll was taken from early June through the last polls taken before the election. To minimize the problem of incompatible poll results, only those polls that sampled registered voters were used in the analysis. Second, the poll results were averaged by day, yielding a single figure for Republican and Democratic candidate support for each day that polling results were available. The difference between the percentage supporting the Republican candidate and the percentage supporting the Democratic candidate (Republican percentage – Democratic percentage) was then calculated and used as the dependent variable. The data in Table A.1 illustrate how the dependent variable was calculated for June 6 to June 8, based on the results of a Gallup poll taken from June 6 to June 8 and a *Washington Post/ABC News* poll taken from June 6 to June 7.

The days for which polling data are not available present a special problem. Rather than exclude these days from the analysis, poll values are estimated for these days by interpolating between days with existing data. For example, if the polling data give a Republican advantage of 6 percentage points on one day and 8 percentage points two days later, and there are no data available for the middle day, an interpolated value of 7 percentage points would be assigned to the middle day.

Table A.2   Accuracy of Last-Day Polling Results

	1984	1988	1992
Last day poll advantage	+20.0	+10.5	−5.5
Actual outcome	+18.2	+7.8	−5.6
Difference	−1.8	−2.7	+0.1

NOTE: Entries are the net Republican percentage-point advantage over the Democratic candidate.

On any given day these trial-heat results represent the relative level of support for the major-party candidates. Although it is difficult to demonstrate that these results represent the actual vote intention of respondents, some indication of the accuracy of these data can be gleaned by comparing the estimated outcome based on the last-day polling results to the actual election outcome. As the data in Table A.2 indicate, the last-day polling results are an accurate reflection of the actual election outcome, especially for the 1984 and 1992 elections. One important implication of this close relationship between the poll results and the actual election outcomes is that any model that generates an accurate prediction of the last-day polling result is also generating a close prediction of the actual election outcome (see Chapter 6).

Appendix B

Debate Surveys

All surveys used in the individual-level analysis in Chapter 5 were conducted by *CBS News* and the *New York Times* and were obtained through the Inter-University Consortium for Political and Social Research (ICPSR). All surveys were conducted by telephone and all samples were drawn using random-digit dialing. Analyses of these surveys included a weighting variable that weighted on the basis of region, race, and gender. The surveys each included a predebate battery of questions on a wide variety of topics related to the election and a postdebate battery of questions focusing on the respondents' reactions to the debates.

The survey used for the first debate of 1984 is *CBS News/New York Times National and Local Surveys, Part 11: First Presidential Debate* (ICPSR #8399). The dates of the predebate interviews are September 30 through October 4 and the dates for the postdebate interviews are October 7 and October 9. The survey used for the second debate of 1984 is *CBS News/New*

York Times National and Local Surveys, Part 12: Second Presidential Debate (ICPSR #8399). The predebate interviews were conducted between October 14 and October 17 and the postdebate interviews were conducted on October 21, October 24, and October 25. In both postdebate surveys, all respondents—debate viewers and nonviewers—were asked about their impressions of the debates.

The survey used for the first debate of 1988 is *CBS News/New York Times First Presidential Debate Panel Survey, September 1988* (ICPSR #9143). The predebate interviews were conducted on September 21 and September 22 and the postdebate interviews were conducted on September 25. The survey used for the second debate in 1988 is *CBS News/New York Times Second Presidential Debate Panel Survey, October 1988* (ICPSR #9147). Predebate interviews were conducted between October 8 and October 10 and postdebate interviews were conducted on October 13. Only debate viewers were asked their impression of the debate in the postdebate interview.

The survey used for the first debate of 1992 is *CBS News/New York Times Monthly Poll #1, October 1992* (ICPSR #6091). The predebate interviews were conducted between October 2 and October 4 and the postdebate interviews were conducted on October 11. Only debate viewers were asked for their impressions of the debate in the postdebate survey.

Appendix C

Alternative Models

One would be remiss if certain design issues concerning the method of analysis used here were not brought up. The first issue concerns the degree to which this design is truly dynamic in nature—that is, the degree to which one can be confident that the results reflect the degree to which the independent variables influence *changes* in the dependent variable. Even though the data analyzed here represent differences in the dependent variable over time, the analysis is still open to being described as essentially static in nature because the values do not represent the actual change in candidate support from one day to the next. One of the more stringent tests for dynamic causality involves including a lagged value of the dependent variable as an independent variable. Doing this allows inferences to be made about the effect of the independent variables while controlling for the effect of previous levels of the dependent variable.

When the model in Table 6.4 is modified to include candidate support in $t - 1$ as an independent variable, the substantive interpretation of the results changes very little (Table C.1). As might be expected, the explanatory power of the model increases substantially and the size of all other coefficients is reduced in the presence of the lagged dependent variable. However, there were very few changes in terms of which variables are significantly related to the dependent variable. The one exception to this is the third debate in 1992, which became significant when the lagged dependent variable was added to the model. More important, the relative effect of each of the independent variables remains essentially intact.

One other possible problem with this analysis lies in the potential for endogeneity among the independent variables. Specifically, it is possible that levels of presidential popularity and consumer sentiment, which are used to measure national conditions, could be influenced by campaign events and campaign rhetoric (see Shaw 1995). If this is the case, then some of the effect being attributed to national conditions may actually reflect the effect of campaigns on perceptions of the president and the state of the economy. One simple method for obviating the potential effect of endogeneity is to measure national conditions just before the campaign actually begins and use this as a constant value for national conditions during the campaign period. Events occurring during the campaign cannot possibly influence perceptions of national conditions prior to the campaign. The only problem with using the May national conditions variable is that it creates a state of perfect collinearity between national conditions and the year dummy variables. This problem is easily resolved by dropping the 1984 dummy variable from the analysis. When the model in Table 6.4 is modified to include only the value of national conditions in May of the election year, very few changes occur in the values of the other coefficients (Table C.2). In fact, one of the few changes that does occur is an increase in the size of the coefficient for national conditions. If endogeneity is a problem, it probably serves to dampen the effect of national conditions.

Table C.1   A Dynamic Model of Candidate Support With a Lagged Dependent
Variable, 1984-1992 (GLS Results)

Variable	b	t-Score
Constant	−16.90	−3.05**
Support $t-1$	.67	18.72**
Conventions		
Democratic, 1984	−1.03	−2.10**
Republican, 1984	1.64	3.12**
Democratic, 1988	−2.02	−3.42**
Republican, 1988	4.26	5.36**
Democratic, 1992	−5.15	−3.12**
Republican, 1992	2.10	3.76**
Debates		
First, 1984	−.63	−.95
Second, 1984	1.84	2.45**
First, 1988	.07	.11
Second, 1988	1.51	2.34**
First, 1992	−1.04	−.92
Second, 1992	−.75	−.56
Third, 1992	2.22	2.01**
Perot	1.24	1.83*
Campaign events	.25	2.08**
Momentum	.06	2.43**
National variables		
External events	.18	.69
Political and economic climate	.24	3.16**
Year effects		
1984	−.70	−.44
1988	−6.87	−3.94**

NOTE: The data have been corrected for first-order autocorrelation using the Yule-Walker procedure. The
estimated value of first-order autocorrelation (prior to correction) is .15.
$R^2 = .98$; $SE = 1.72$; $N = 445$.
*$p < .10$; **$p < .05$.

Table C.2   Model of Candidate Support With June National Conditions, 1984-1992 (GLS Results)

Variable	b	t-Score
Constant	−61.86	−10.01**
Conventions		
Democratic, 1984	−1.84	−1.66*
Republican, 1984	5.81	5.52**
Democratic, 1988	−2.28	−1.99**
Republican, 1988	11.40	8.59**
Democratic, 1992	−13.06	−9.19**
Republican, 1992	6.07	5.66**
Debates		
First, 1984	−1.25	−.95
Second, 1984	5.32	3.64**
First, 1988	.01	.01
Second, 1988	3.26	2.45**
First, 1992	−2.49	−1.47
Second, 1992	−1.76	−.98
Third, 1992	3.44	2.02**
Perot	6.76	6.49**
Campaign events	.73	3.45**
Momentum	.16	4.86**
National variables		
External events	−.39	−.96
Political and economic climate	.83	11.81**
Year effects		
1988	−17.67	−15.04**

NOTE: The data have been corrected for first-order autocorrelation using the Yule-Walker procedure. The estimated value of first-order autocorrelation (prior to correction) is .65.
$R^2 = .85$; $SE = 1.92$; $N = 446$.
*$p < .10$; **$p < .05$.

References

Abramowitz, Alan. 1988. An improved model for predicting presidential elections. *PS* 21:843-47.

Abramson, Paul, John Aldrich, and David Rohde. 1990. *Change and continuity in the 1988 elections.* Washington, DC: CQ Press.

Achen, Christopher. 1982. *Interpreting and using regression.* Beverly Hills, CA: Sage.

Aldrich, John H. 1980. *Before the convention: Strategies and choices in presidential nominating campaigns.* Chicago: University of Chicago Press.

———. 1993. Presidential selection. In *Researching the presidency,* edited by George C. Edwards III, John H. Kessel, and Bert A. Rockman. Pittsburgh, PA: University of Pittsburgh Press.

Allsop, Dee, and Herbert F. Weisberg. 1988. Measuring change in party identification in an election campaign. *American Journal of Political Science* 32:996-1017.

American Enterprise. 1992. Public opinion and demographic report. *The public perspective: A Roper Center review of public opinion and polling.* November/December:100-01.

American National Election Studies Cumulative Data File, 1952-1992 (ICPSR #8475). Ann Arbor: University of Michigan, Center for Political Studies.

American National Election Studies Cumulative Data File, 1952-1992 (ICPSR #5475). Ann Arbor: University of Michigan, Center for Political Studies.

Ansolabehere, Stephen, Roy Behr, and Shanto Iyengar. 1993. *The media game.* New York: Macmillan.

Apple, R. W., Jr. 1992. Behind Bush's mixed abortion signals. *New York Times,* August 15, A1.

Arcelus, Francisco, and Allan Meltzer. 1975. The effect of aggregate economic conditions on Congressional elections. *American Political Science Review* 69:1232-39.

Bartels, Larry M. 1988. *Presidential primaries and the dynamics of public choice.* Princeton, NJ: Princeton University Press.

———. 1992. The impact of electioneering in the United States. In *Electioneering: A comparative study of continuity and change,* edited by David Butler and Austin Ranney. Oxford, UK: Clarendon.

————. 1993. Messages received: The political impact of media exposure. *American Political Science Review* 87:267-85.

Bloom, Howard, and H. Douglas Price. 1975. Voter response to short-run economic conditions: The asymmetric effect of prosperity and recession. *American Political Science Review* 69: 1240-54.

Boyd, Gerald. 1984. Jackson charges he was ignored for the No. 2 spot. *New York Times,* July 11, A1.

Brunk, Gregory, and Paul Gough. 1983. State-level economic conditions and the 1980 presidential election. *Presidential Studies Quarterly* 13:62-9.

Campbell, Angus, Philip E. Converse, Warren E. Miller, and Donald E. Stokes. 1960. *The American voter.* New York: John Wiley.

Campbell, James E. 1992. Forecasting the presidential vote in the States. *American Journal of Political Science* 36:386-407.

Campbell, James E., Lynne Cherry, and Kenneth Wink. 1992. The convention bump. *American Politics Quarterly* 20:287-307.

Campbell, James E., and Kenneth Wink. 1990. Trial-heat forecasts of the presidential vote. *American Politics Quarterly* 18:251-69.

CBS News/New York Times First Presidential Debate Panel Survey, September 1988 (ICPSR #9143). Ann Arbor: University of Michigan, Center for Political Studies.

CBS News/New York Times Monthly Poll #1, October 1992 (ICPSR #6091). Ann Arbor: University of Michigan, Center for Political Studies.

CBS News/New York Times National and Local Surveys, Part 11: First Presidential Debate (ICPSR #8399). Ann Arbor: University of Michigan, Center for Political Studies.

CBS News/New York Times National and Local Surveys, Part 12: Second Presidential Debate (ICPSR #8399). Ann Arbor: University of Michigan, Center for Political Studies.

CBS News/New York Times Second Presidential Debate Panel Survey, October 1988 (ICPSR #9147). Ann Arbor: University of Michigan, Center for Political Studies.

Congressional Quarterly. 1987. *National party conventions.* Washington, DC: Congressional Quarterly.

Converse, Philip E. 1966. The concept of the normal vote. In *Elections and the political order,* edited by Angus Campbell, Warren E. Miller, and Donald E. Stokes. New York: John Wiley.

Darnay, Arsen. 1994. *Economic indicators handbook.* Detroit, MI: Gale Research.

DeMaris, Alfred. 1993. *Logit modeling: Practical applications.* London: Sage.

Denton, Robert E., Jr., and Mary E. Stuckey. 1994. A communication model of presidential campaigns: A 1992 overview. In *The 1992 presidential campaign: A communication perspective,* edited by Robert E. Denton, Jr. Westport, CT: Praeger.

Downs, Anthony. 1957. *An economic theory of democracy.* New York: Harper & Row.

Edwards, George C. III, and Alec Gallup. 1990. *Presidential approval: A sourcebook.* Baltimore, MD: Johns Hopkins University Press.

Facts on file. 1984. New York: Facts on File.

Facts on file. 1988. New York: Facts on File.

Facts on file. 1992. New York: Facts on File.

Fair, Ray C. 1978. The effect of economic events on votes for president. *Review of Economics and Statistics* 60:159-72.

Finkel, Steven. 1993. Reexamining the "minimal effects" model in recent presidential elections. *Journal of Politics* 55:1-21.

Fiorina, Morris. 1981. *Retrospective voting in American national elections.* New Haven, CT: Yale University Press.

Geer, John G. 1988. The effects of presidential debates on the electorate's preferences for candidates. *American Politics Quarterly* 16:486-501.

Gelman, Andrew, and Gary King. 1993. Why are American presidential election polls so variable when votes are so predictable? *British Journal of Political Science* 23:409-51.

Germond, Jack, and Jules Witcover. 1985. *Wake us when it's over: Presidential politics in 1984.* New York: Macmillan.

———. 1989. *Whose broad stripes and bright stars? The trivial pursuit of the presidency 1988.* New York: Warner.

Goldman, Peter, Thomas DeFrank, Mark Miller, Andrew Murr, and Tom Mathews. 1994. *Quest for the presidency: 1992.* College Station: University of Texas Press.

Goldman, Peter, Tony Fuller, et al. 1985. *The quest for the presidency: The 1984 campaign.* New York: Bantam.

Goldman, Peter, Tom Mathews, et al. 1989. *The quest for the presidency: The 1988 campaign.* New York: Touchstone.

Goodman, Saul, and Gerald Kramer. 1975. Commentary on Arcelus and Meltzer: The effect of aggregate economic conditions on Congressional elections. *American Political Science Review* 69:1255-65.

Hanushek, Eric, and John Jackson. 1977. *Statistical methods for social scientists.* New York: Academic Press.

Hellinger, Daniel, and Dennis R. Judd. 1991. *The democratic facade.* Pacific Grove, CA: Brooks/Cole.

Hershey, Marjorie Randon. 1989. The campaign and the media. In *The election of 1988: Reports and interpretations,* edited by Gerald Pomper. Chatham, NJ: Chatham House.

Hibbs, Douglas A. 1982. President Reagan's mandate from the 1980 elections: A shift to the right? *American Politics Quarterly* 10:387-420.

Holbrook, Thomas M. 1991. Presidential elections in space and time. *American Journal of Political Science* 35:91-109.

———. 1994. The behavioral consequences of vice-presidential debates: Does the undercard have any punch? *American Politics Quarterly* 22:469-82.

Jamieson, Kathleen Hall. 1992. *Packaging the presidency,* 2nd ed. Oxford, UK: Oxford University Press.

Jamieson, Kathleen Hall, and David Birdsell. 1988. *Presidential debates: The challenge of creating an informed electorate.* New York: Oxford University Press.

Key, V. O., Jr. 1966. *The responsible electorate.* Cambridge, MA: Belknap.

Kiewiet, D. Roderick, and Douglas Rivers. 1985. The economic basis of Reagan's appeal. In *The new direction in American politics,* edited by John E. Chubb and Paul E. Peterson. Washington, DC: Brookings Institution.

Kinder, Donald, Gordon Adams, and Paul Gronke. 1989. Economics and politics in the 1984 presidential election. *American Political Science Review* 33:491-515.

Kramer, Gerald H. 1971. Short-term fluctuations in U.S. voting behavior, 1896-1964. *American Political Science Review* 65:131-43.

Kraus, Sidney, and Dennis K. Davis. 1981. Political debates. In *The handbook of political communication,* edited by D. Nimmo and K. Sanders. Beverly Hills, CA: Sage.

Lanoue, David J. 1991. The "turning point": Viewers' reactions to the second 1988 presidential debate. *American Politics Quarterly* 19:80-95.

———. 1992. One that made a difference: Cognitive consistency, political knowledge, and the 1980 presidential debate. *Public Opinion Quarterly* 56:168-84.

Lanoue, David, and Peter Schrott. 1991. *The joint press conference.* New York: Greenwood.

Lau, Richard R. 1995. Information search during an election campaign: Introducing a processing-tracing methodology for political scientists. In *Political judgement: Structure and process,* edited by Milton Lodge and Kathleen McGraw. Ann Arbor: University of Michigan Press.

Lazarsfeld, Paul, Bernard Berelson, and Helen Gaudet. 1944. *The people's choice.* New York: Duell, Sloane, & Pearce.

Lemert, James, William Elliott, James Bernstein, William Rosenberg, and Karl Nestvold. 1991. *News verdicts, the debates, and presidential campaigns.* New York: Praeger.

Lewis-Beck, Michael. 1986. Interrupted time series. In *New tools for social scientists,* edited by William D. Berry and Michael S. Lewis-Beck. Beverly Hills, CA: Sage.

———. 1988. Economics and the American voter: Past, present, future. *Political Behavior* 10:5-21.

Lewis-Beck, Michael, and Tom Rice. 1992. *Forecasting elections.* Washington, DC: CQ Press.

Li, Richard P. Y. 1976. A dynamic comparative analysis of presidential and House elections. *American Journal of Political Science* 20:671-91.

Liesner, Thelma. 1989. *One hundred years of economic statistics.* New York: Facts on File.

Light, Paul, and Celinda Lake. 1985. The Election: Candidates, Strategies, and Decisions. In *The Elections of 1984,* edited by Michael Nelson. Washington, DC: CQ Press.

Lodge, Milton, Kathleen McGraw, and Patrick Stroh. 1989. An impression-driven model of candidate evaluation. *American Political Science Review* 87:399-419.

Lodge, Milton, Marco Steenbergen, and Shawn Brau. 1995. The responsive voter: Campaign information and the dynamics of candidate evaluation. *American Political Science Review* 89: 309-26.

Lodge, Milton, and Patrick Stroh. 1993. Inside the mental voting booth: An impression-driven model of candidate evaluation. In *Explorations in political psychology,* edited by Shanto Iyengar and William J. McGuire. Durham, NC: Duke University Press.

Markus, Gregory B. 1988. The impact of personal and national economic conditions on the presidential vote: A pooled cross-sectional analysis. *American Journal of Political Science* 32:137-54.

Markus, Gregory, and Philip Converse. 1979. A dynamic simultaneous equation model of electoral choice. *American Political Science Review* 73:617-32.

Moore, Jonathan, ed. 1986. *Campaign for president: The managers look at '84.* Dover, MA: Auburn House.

Nadeau, Richard, Richard G. Niemi, and Timothy Amato. 1994. Expectations and preferences in British general elections. *American Political Science Review* 88:371-83.

Oreskes, Michael. 1988. Jackson, "too mature" for anger, icily offers no embrace for ticket. *New York Times,* July 13, A1.

Owen, Diana. 1991. *Media messages in American presidential elections.* New York: Greenwood.

Page, Benjamin, and Calvin Jones. 1979. Reciprocal effects of policy preferences, party loyalties, and the vote. *American Political Science Review* 73:1071-89.

Patterson, Thomas E. 1989. The press and its missed assignment. In *The elections of 1988,* edited by Michael Nelson. Washington, DC: CQ Press.

Pomper, Gerald, ed. 1985. *The election of 1984: Reports and Interpretations.* Chatham, NJ: Chatham House.

———. ed. 1989. *The election of 1988: Reports and interpretations.* Chatham, NJ: Chatham House.

Popkin, Samuel. 1991. *The reasoning voter: Communication and persuasion in presidential campaigns.* Chicago: University of Chicago Press.

Quirk, Paul, and Jon K. Dalager. 1993. The election: A "new Democrat" and a new kind of presidential campaign. In *The elections of 1992,* edited by Michael Nelson. Washington, DC: CQ Press.

Rosenstone, Steven. 1983. *Forecasting presidential elections.* New Haven, CT: Yale University Press.

————. 1985. Why Reagan won. *Brookings Review* 3:25-32.

Runkel, David. 1989. *Campaign for president: The managers look at '88.* Dover, MA: Auburn House.

Salmore, Barbara, and Stephen Salmore. 1989. *Candidates, parties, and campaigns,* 2d ed. Washington, DC: CQ Press.

Shaw, Daron. 1995. Strong persuasion? The effect of campaigns in U.S. presidential elections. Ph.D. dissertation, University of California, Los Angeles.

Shelley, Mack C. II, and Hwang-Du Hwang. 1991. The mass media and public opinion polls in the 1988 presidential election. *American Politics Quarterly* 19:59-79.

Shively, W. Phillips. 1992. From differential abstention to conversion: A change in electoral change, 1864-1988. *American Journal of Political Science* 36:309-30.

Skalaban, Andrew. 1988. Do the polls affect elections? Some 1980 evidence. *Political Behavior* 10:136-50.

Stanley, Harold, and Richard G. Niemi. 1992. *Vital statistics on American politics,* 3d ed. Washington, DC: CQ Press.

————. 1994. *Vital statistics on American politics,* 4th ed. Washington, DC: CQ Press.

Stimson, James. 1985. Regression in space and time: A statistical essay. *American Journal of Political Science* 29:914-47.

Traugott, Michael. 1992. The impact of media polls on the public. In *Media polls in American politics,* edited by Thomas E. Mann and Gary Orren. Washington, DC: Brookings Institution.

Tufte, Edward R. 1978. *Political control of the economy.* Princeton, NJ: Princeton University Press.

Wattenberg, Martin P. 1990. *The decline of American political parties, 1952-1988.* Cambridge, MA: Harvard University Press.

————. 1991. *The rise of candidate-centered politics.* Cambridge, MA: Harvard University Press.

Wayne, Stephen J. 1992. *The road to the White House 1992: The politics of presidential elections.* New York: St. Martin's.

Weisberg, Herbert F., and Dee Allsop. 1990. Sources of short-term change in party identification. Paper presented at the annual meeting of the Midwest Political Science Association, Chicago, April.

Weisman, Steven R. 1984. G.O.P. worry: Wooing viewers. *New York Times,* July 22, A1.

West, Darrell M. 1993. *Air wars: Television advertising in election campaigns, 1952-1992.* Washington, DC: CQ Press.

Index

About the Author

Thomas M. Holbrook is Associate Professor of Political Science at the University of Wisconsin—Milwaukee. He has published articles on elections and state politics in the *American Political Science Review, American Journal of Political Science, Journal of Politics,* and several other political science journals.